Yorkshire Laughter

A tale efther it's been tell'd by
three Yorkshiremen owt to start
frae scratch again.

(Anon).

T'owd tongue gives mooth.
Neean eeasy ta read er write t'day,
But easy as winking, lads, t'say!

(John Thwaite, of Wensleydale).

Gi'e us, Lord, a bit o' sun,
A bit o' wark, a bit o' fun.
Gi' us all, in t'struggle an' splutter,
Our daily bread—and a bit o' butter.

(Anon).

Yorkshire Laughter

NATIVE WIT AND HUMOUR

by

W R Mitchell

Foreword by Freddie Trueman, OBE
Cover and drawings by Ionicus

CASTLEBERG
1992

for

CAROL LAMBERT

and the staff of J W Lambert and Sons,
Printers, Settle (in the firm's centenary year).

Published by Castleberg, 18 Yealand Avenue, Giggleswick,
Settle, North Yorkshire, BD24 0AY

Typeset in Clearface and printed by J W Lambert & Sons,
Station Road, Settle, North Yorkshire, BD24 9AA

ISBN: 1 871064 85 6

Foreword

by Freddie Trueman, OBE

(who for 20 years played in Yorkshire and Test cricket)

MY favourite Yorkshire story is, naturally, about cricket.

It was the first day of a county match, Yorkshire versus Glamorgan, at Harrogate.

An old-age pensioner went along to pay his membership subscription, and he and the secretary chatted about the good weather.

Said the secretary: "You'd have thought there'd be more people in the ground on a lovely day like this".

The pensioner remarked: "I wouldn't worry; it'll fill up after lunch".

The secretary asked why this should be, and the pensioner replied: "It's half-day closing at Pateley Bridge".

All good wishes to Bill Mitchell's book of humorous tales.

WHEN I chatted with James Gregson at his retirement home in Grassington, he defined the best type of Yorkshire story as one that has wit, brevity [the soul of wit], humour and realism, with a homely, down-to-earth presentation. His favourite, incorporating all those qualities, was: "Nivver put thi husband on a pedestal. He'll nobbut need dusting".

Introduction

YORKSHIRE folk, of all shapes, sizes, colours and creeds, are bound together by—county pride.

The archetypal "Ee by Gum" Yorkshireman, a rather brash milltown type, with cap, muffler and tyke [a small dog], was a creation of the 19th century music hall and dialect writers.

Today, the "typical" Yorkshireman comes from south of Leeds and glories in his broad accents and forthright manner, which makes a refreshing change from plummy BBC English.

There are other types, and quieter forms of speech, in the huge and varied county of Yorkshire, which an American described to me as "a sort of Texas of England".

You will also find Yorkshire-by-the-Sea, Yorkshire-on-the-Moors (and Wolds), and the Yorkshire of the Vale and Plain.

Then there's the Yorkshire of the Pennine Dales. Before the Boundary Commission played fast and loose with our western border, Yorkshire extended to within 16 miles of the Irish Sea, giving our old rival, Lancashire, a waist like a wasp.

As far as I am concerned, the boundary is as it ever was. Our neighbours have just got bits of it on loan.

Off-comers do not always appreciate that daftness is one of our Yorkshire family jokes. You will have heard that at Cowling and elsewhere men tried to rake t'moon out of a mill dam or (at Austwick) they walled in a cuckoo to keep good weather in the village.

Television has played havoc with Yorkshire traditions. Fictional series have created several mini-districts which are real to many viewers but have no official recognition. South Country scriptwriters, actors and actresses have diluted the Yorkshire character, which had been so well upheld by such as J B Priestley and James R Gregson.

Coach proprietors organise trips to the "Herriot Country" (Swaledale/Wensleydale), with TV programmes based originally on the best-selling (and authentic) books of James Herriot. Then there's "Constable Country" (this Constable being not the famous landscape artist but a policeman who chases wrongdoers across the North York Moors.

"The Last of the Summer Wine" Country came into being when a BBC producer, clutching a very funny script, fixed on Holmfirth, in the West Riding, as the location of a series. (The writer had not had any specific town in mind when he devised and wrote this successful series). The locale for "Emmerdale Farm" is Esholt, on the outskirts of Bradford. (Esholt had been internationally famous for its high-tech sewage works).

Yorkshire folk are rather dour, though it costs nowt to smile. Yet Yorkshire is a very funny place. Telling amusing tales is a county-wide occupation, whether the teller lives in Whitby or Waddington.

The stories they tell are mainly connected with our large Yorkshire family. Off-comers originally feel left-out. Traditionally, those unfortunate enough to have been born outside Yorkshire are "wintered and summered and wintered again" before being accepted. Now, in many rural areas, they greatly outnumber the natives and have brought their city ways, such as barbecues, to what had been quiet little villages.

Yorkshire wit is that spontaneous re-action to a situation which does not allow for much thought. Humour, on the other hand, is contrived, anecdotal, reflective.

Here's an example of Yorkshire wit. In the 1914-18 war, a recruiting sergeant visited a Dales village and saw a milkman on his rounds. "Would you like to serve the King," boomed the sergeant. "Aye," he replied enthusiastically, "but I can nobbut spare a pint today".

Humour is evident in the story of two men who were walking on Whitby beach when one picked up a piece of the hard, black substance known as jet and said: "This is powerful stuff; I hear tell they're running aeroplanes off it now".

Some of the best Yorkshire humour has an element of self-mockery, even of simple mindedness. The folk of Slaithwaite (pronounced Slawit) are known as Moonrakers, from the time some were supposed to have seen the reflection of the moon in the canal which runs between Marsden and Huddersfield. They thought it was a sunken cheese and tried to rake it out.

The folk of Marsden, at the head of the valley, are known as Cuckoos. They share with Austwick that daft story about building a wall around the roosting place of a cuckoo in the hope of retaining it and thereby enjoying perpetual summer.

Do not be decided by the apparent gormlessness of the Moonrakers. Perhaps they were "acting daft" so that the revenue men would not detect their stock of illicit spirit, which they had hastily sunk in t'cut.

The farmer at Hawes who has a cow to sell or the millowner at Bradford who is negotiating a price for the world's best woollen cloth may have bland expressions on their face, but each mind is as sharp and nimble as a computer. Each, in the end, comes out best in a bargain.

Yorkshire humour is at times self-deprecating. A Yorkshireman who "passed over" found himself on the threshold of Heaven. St Peter, having discovered his place of origin, said: "Thou can come in, lad, but we're not makkin' Yorkshire pudding for one".

A crusty, miserly Yorkshireman found himself (much to his surprise) in Heaven. In the same celestrial room was an attractive young woman. He asked St Peter if this was a reward for years well spent on earth. "No," said St Peter. "It's her punishment".

A Dales farmer who was "fading" was asked by pious relatives to give their good wishes to various people, family and friends, who had gone before. With his last breath, the old farmer said: "Does ta think I'll have nowt better to do in Heaven than go clomping about looking for thy Jack, Fred and Mary?"

No one actually dies in Yorkshire. My father's favourite story was about the woman who "lost" her husband and she had an inscribed stone put up at the grave. On it were the letters RIP, signifying "Rest in Peace". When she began to hear things about him and other women, she asked the monumental mason to carve, after RIP, the words "Till I Come".

Yorkshire humour is realistic. My father-in-law, a farmer, had some good tales, including that of the farmer who sold a horse. The buyer returned and said: "Yon hoss is no good. It wean't hold its head up". Said the buyer: "It's that hoss's pride, lad. Thee get it paid for!"

In the textile area, the operative who kept dozing off was sacked. He was back at work the next morning. The overlooker said: "I thowt I sacked you". "Aye," was the laconic reply, "but that were yesterda'."

The man who repeatedly arrived late was shouted at by the boss, who said: "Na then, you knaw what time we start work at this mill". "Nay, I doan't," he replied. "Everybody's already warking when I turn up".

The weaver's wife said to her husband on his return from work: "Did you like your sandwiches? I made you a special sort" He looked bemused, then said: "Eh—to tell you t'truth, I forgot to look in 'em".

There's a grimness about some Yorkshire stories. A man who had a painful illness said, despairingly, to his wife: "Ay, lass, I'd tak poison if I thowt it'd do me onny good".

The Dalesman magazine, with which I was associated for over four decades, served up a regular diet of traditional Yorkshire stories—and, I suspect, some tales from other areas which had been "traditionalised". They were sent in by our readers.

Only once did I use a pornographic joke and that was about the two farmers who met in Skipton. While conversing, one said: "What's ta think about all this pornography?" The reply was: "Nay—I doan't knaw. I hevn't getten a pornograph".

It's How You Tell 'Em

YOU WILL possibly have heard of the newcomer to Armley Gaol. He was intriqued when, every now and then, someone in the cell block shouted a number and there was general laughter. His cell-mate explained that the jokes had been "cracked" so often that each had been given a number to save time and trouble.

He shouted: "Thirty-two". There was no response. He yelled: "Forty-eight". Silence followed. His cell-mate remarked: "It all depends on how you tell 'em".

Much depends on the audience. I usually test the temperature with what I consider to be an amusing story before getting down to business. Sometimes, after a Dales talk, a Dales farmer approaches me and says: "We can't be as daft as thou maks out". I tell him that all my best Dales farmer jokes have been told me by—Dales farmers.

The most popular of the tales I have told, judging by the applause at countless talks, concerns the old man who was "fading". He asked for a candle to brighten his last hours. His thrifty wife said: "Nay, lad—thou knaws t'price o' candles". He persisted and his wife relented. As she left the room, she said: "If thou feels thissen going, blow t'candle out".

Another of similar type relates to Ben Hudson, of Clapham, who looked every inch a dalesman, with his tweedy clothes, cloth cap and leather boots. He had a weather-seamed face which had about it the grandeur of an Old Testament prophet. Ben was just the man to ask about the state of the weather.

"What's the weather doing to do, Ben?"

He looked at the sky for a minute or two; he looked at the

beck for another minute and then appeared to be looking at his feet. In due course, he turned and said:

"It could do owt".

Rigging up a projector was an entertainment in itself, especially if it was as battered as mine and the only available support (as in the large Victoria Hall, Settle) was a metal step-ladder, two legs resting on bricks, with the projector perched on top and angled with the help of some beer mats. The whole was tied on for safety using a scarf borrowed from a member of the audience.

Introductions could be unhelpful. A chairlady said: "I am deputising for Mrs Smith, who is on holiday in America. I am sure we all wish we could be with her..."

I heard the apocryphal tale of a chairperson who reminded the members that she had been asked to get "a celebrated wit" for the next meeting. She had failed and so had arranged for the presence of two half-wits!

I have sat through discussions on the high cost of lecturers (I charged nowt) and on the poor quality of lecturers. At a women's organisation there were so many reports that my contribution began an hour and a half late—and I was asked to cut it down to a quarter of an hour.

At a farmer's get-together at Burnsall, in Wharfedale, I used all the good stories, but the best-sustained round of laughter came from the man who proposed the vote of thanks. He said: "I'm not a talker, so I'm not going to say much. Shall I tell thee a story?"

But of course...

"Nay, there were this owd lady who got fed-up living in a retirement home. She was fed-up because every day was like t'last..."

The farmer who said he wasn't "much of a hand" at talking developed his tale in masterly style. The old lady in the retirement home said to a friend—another old lady—that she was bahn to mak things more exciting by stripping off and streaking through t'lounge. Which she did.

As she passed out of the room into the hall, two short-sighted old men looked at her. One said: "Was that Betty?" Said the other: "Nay, I don't know—but whoever it was, her dress needs ironing".

Invariably, after a talk, someone comes up with a Yorkshire tale to tell. Sometimes, it is a well-known story, related at length. There are delectable moments when the humour is at first hand, as at Sedbergh, against a backdrop of the Howgill Fells.

Here I spoke to a meeting organised by farmers' wives; they had invited the public to attend.

An old lady afterwards recalled when someone wishing to live at Sedbergh was unable to do so because there was no suitable house. A local man said: "Thee wait till winter. 'Appen somebody'll dee".

At another meeting, the subject swung to local doctors, one of whom did not seem very quick on the uptake. "Aye", said a native of the town, "Dr ----- is a good 'un. Go to t'other fellow with your head under your arm and he'll ask—what seems to be the matter?"

Ill-health usually cropped up in conversation before a meeting began as the chairwoman acquainted me with the ailments of some of the more exceptional members—such as the ancient lady with the "new hip" who had just been sponsored to walk a mile or the ultra thin lady who, if she had a cup of tea, must surely resemble a thermometer. This lady was indomitable. "You wouldn't think that t'doctor had given her up two months ago . . . She's going to Bridlington for a holiday next week".

Medical talk always reminded me of the story I heard at Whitby—of the young doctor who told an elderly patient he could find nothing wrong with her. She snorted and said: "Young man, I was in failing health before you were born".

Tales of ill-health are numberless. A York doctor who prescrib-ed a mustard plaster was ill-prepared for the reaction of the patient who had found it was "too hot to eat".

An improbable but entertaining yarn concerns a mother who rang the doctor to report her son had swallowed her fountain pen. The doctor asked what she was doing about it, and she replied: "I'm using a ball-point".

After talking for an hour and a-half, I am rarely in the mood for a long conversation. Many years ago, when I had talked to Methodists in York, I stayed overnight at the home of the City Engineer, Mr Minter.

He was fond of Yorkshire humour, but wisely jotted down catch-lines to remind him of the best tales. While sipping cups of coffee at his home, we began to exchange tales. It was in the wee small hours that we crept to our beds.

He had concluded with the story of the farmer from a village on the Plain who brought his young son to York for the day. At one stage of the tour, he rapped the end of his walking stick on a pavement and said: "I'll tell thee why you don't find many folk farming in York. . . Grund's too hard to plough".

A DALES couple arrived at a bank with a bucketful of sovereigns. The cashier was asked to count the coins, which she did, announcing that the bucket held 2,376 sovereigns. The man, looking unhappy, asked for a re-count. The cashier obliged, with the same result. The dalesman turned to his wife and said: "Nay, lass—we've browt t'wrong bucket".

Aircraft

YORKSHIRE folk used to look up when they heard a plane droning over. Now, a military jet passes at zero feet, with a whine and a whoosh, and no one takes a bit of notice. The sheep carry on grazing. Even the hens, the most nervous of farm stock, keep calm.

A farmer's wife in Wensleydale told me she likes to see a low-flying jet and rushes out of the house when she hears one coming. Her husband told me of the dalesman who read in t'*Yorkshire Post* that an aircraft had got into difficulty and the pilot had to bale out.

"Aye," said the dalesman, "tha can allus learn summat. I nivver knew they carried that much watter wi' 'em".

The tourist jet aircraft no longer scares people. Holidaymakers clamber on to it with the nonchalance they used to feel when catching a bus. A woman had a holiday in Tenerife. Her friend asked: "Where's Tenerife?" The reply was: "Nay, I've no idea. We went by plane".

A "common" type of woman who had "married brass" and improved herself materially to the extent of having a fine bungalow, a posh car and overseas holidays, set out to impress her old friends. After one trip abroad, by air, she invited them to her home. Lower jaws drooped in astonishment at the sight of such luxury. "What about rates?" said a friend. "We hev no rates," was the reply, "just a few mace but I have bought a trap for them."

Then, continuing to use her posh voice, she described the holiday: "We flew to Crete; we got out of the aeroplane, looked at the hills and—we was fair capped". Which is the old Yorkshire expression for "impressed".

Milltown Speyks

I CAMPED [visited for a chat] that celebrated broadcaster, James R Gregson, and we yarned about matters Yorkshire. He was my favourite raconteur and his Yorkshire plays held some pithy "speyks", such as:

Ah can read him better na big print.
also
As flustered as a hen that wants to sit.
and
As uneasy as a dog wi' too monny fleas.

Here are some from other sources in industrialised Yorkshire: *It's all bed an' wark.*

Of a severe-looking woman: *She's a face as black as t'fireback.*

Of a wealthy industrialist: *He's that weel off, he's bow-legged wi' brass.*

Other familiar speyks are:

Of a textile operative, on Monday morning: "He's warking on t'deeard hoss [doing work for which he had already been paid]".

Of a long-haired youth: "Mind, when thou passes t'barber's shop that t'pole doesn't tummle on thee".

He's abaart as much good as a soft coppin [a bane in the textile process].

They're as thick [friendly] as Inkle weyvers [Inkles being narrow tapes which were set close together].

Angling

YORKSHIRE has plenty of watter. The Pennines ask for trouble by presenting a big north-south barrier to the westerly weather, with its rain-bearing clouds. If you can see the hills, it's going to rain and if you can't see them, it's raining.

The main rivers, which look on the map like the veins on the back of a leaf, pour water into the Ouse and periodically flood York when there is a general thaw of snow ligging on the fells. It is said at Rathmell, in the Ribble valley, that a farm man fell asleep on a heap of hay. The river, unexpectedly flooding, collected the hay and its passenger. He awoke, saw some men and asked where he was. They replied: "Rathmell". Still dozy from sleep, the voyager asked for confirmation: "Do you mean Rathmell-in-England?"

The high fells, with their peat and sphagnum moss, used to hold water like a sponge and release it gradually. Now, after much gripping [drainage using a special plough] there is one big rush of water and the headwaters often dry out in summer. Hence the story of the angler who tried to impress a friend by saying: "I copped a fish that big, when I took it out, t'beck went down two inches". The beck was probably only four inches deep at the time.

Yorkshire has thousands of anglers. To the older generation two men to be revered are Izaak Walton and W Carter Platts (1858-1944). The latter was born in Huddersfield but lived at Skipton with a dozen tobacco pipes, a typewriter and 1,000 books.

Platts had a breezy, light-hearted style:

"As the driver handed down my impendimenta at the point where the road approached the bend of the river, he opined that the day from a meteorological point of view would ho'd up and wished me good sport. Unfortunately, the day did not ho'd up, and the weather and I arrived at the river almost at the same time".

His books contain many good stories. He told, for example, of a retired West Riding manufacturer who all his life had wanted "a full ha'porth for his ha'penny". He went on a fishing excursion to Scotland, hired a boat and fished a loch.

When many hours had gone by, and he had worked the boatman to the point of exhaustion, he sweetly observed: "There, lads, I think we'll land now and give up for today. We'll start an hour earlier tomorrow to make up for it!"

Tykes [from the West Riding] frequently came across "No Fishing" signs. Two men decided to break with precedent and actually ask permission to fish. They walked up to the big house. The valet made inquiries, returned and said: "His Lordship acquiesces". One of the Yorkshiremen said: "All reet then. We'll go and fish somewhere else".

The angling tales are legion. A man who was told he was fishing in private water said: "Well, I'll stop for a while. Then I'll be fishing water from further up t'dale". At Malham Tarn, where fishing is from a boat, two men did so well that one of them said: "I hope you made a note of the place where we caught the trout". His friend said he had put a cross on the bottom of the boat, whereupon the first man observed: "Don't be daft! We might not get that particular boat tomorn".

Art

YOU have to be sharpish to record our transient weather. Pause to sneeze, and the cloud that took your fancy is a dozen miles to the east. Water-colour, applied in bold washes, is the medium to use. Oil paints allow you to be more reflective.

A well-to-do Bradford artist submitted to *The Dalesman* his painting of "The River Aire at Cottingley", a picture which was somewhat streaky, in the modern style. A reader sent a postcard with her comments about it:

Aire river—nay, nivver!
But it maks no matter, for I can't see t'watter!

Reginald Brundrit, RA., who had a studio in Upper Wharfedale, sent a painting on wood and when it was shattered in the post he charged us £25 compensation—and then inquired what had happened to the bits.

Another artist, who lives in Leeds, has such restless fingers that while waiting for his wife to fill a trolley at the supermarket, he makes a drawing of a Yorkshire scene using spent matches and a blank part of a cigarette packet.

Fred Lawson, who as a young man went to Wensleydale for a week's holiday, and stayed for the rest of his life, produced a drawing which was unlike any he had done before and gave the impression of Impressionism. Fred, when asked to give the drawing a title, wrote: "It's of a bit of loose plaster on the wall of our outside privvy".

A friend who "fancied himself" as a portrait painter, invited me to accompany him to Wensleydale, where he had painted the daughter of a farmer and was now about to deliver the painting. It was an embarrassing occasion. The farmer was full of praise for the artist. He had never seen a better portrait.

There was a pause and he added: "Who is it?"

Realism is undoubtedly one of the characteristics of Yorkshire folk and is evident in an approach to art. It was taken to excess by a farmer who bought an oil painting rather than a water-colour "because there's more paint on it". A sheep picture was chosen rather than another study of sheep "because there's more sheep".

A visiting artist, impressed when a farmer provided him with a sheep that stood for a long time without undue movement, returned the next day, requested the use of the same sheep and marvelled that the farmer could find the same animal in such a large flock. The farmer said: "I reckon thou could tell thy wife amang two hundred other women, couldn't thou?"

The realistic attitude develops at an early age. A farmer's son from the rainy dalehead sat watching as teacher at school helped him out by adding to his picture a lovely blue sky and fluffy white clouds. He then said: "Nay, miss, where I come from, t'clouds is mucky".

They are. On average, 70 inches of rain a year fall on the slates at that remote farm.

Batter Pudding

MOST Yorkshire food for working class families was made to fill bellies cheaply. This mining district variant of *Yorkshire Pudding* clogged up the diner's digestive system so that he or she would not eat too much meat.

Having cooked the Sunday joint, you were left a hot tin and plenty of hot fat. Nowt must go to waste. First make some gravy, pouring some flour over the fat, then some water, stirring it up briskly. Run off the gravy and keep it warm.

The only people who could make batter/Yorkshire Pudding properly were those who had an old-fashioned open range, with fire flanked by oven and water boiler.

The ingredients are the same as for Yorkshire Pudding—flour, egg, milk, some water, then salt, made into a batter—but folk are let down by their modern cookers. For batter pudding, the fat has to be so hot it'll almost melt metal.

Pour the batter in and leave it for about ten minutes. Now open your oven door and lift a corner of the pudding up to see if it is ready. If so, turn it over quickly and slice it into four parts—or however many are going to share it—and cook the other side.

A Yorkshire Pudding rises up and is crisp brown on top. The Batter Pudding is flat and, if you're lucky, about a quarter of an inch thick.

Bedrooms

A WORKING class bedroom was a cheerless place—unheated, with a single hissing gas lamp, lino on the floor and with cold water for washing stored in a jug which stood in a matching bowl.

There are additional hazards in some houses. A West Riding man told a friend he couldn't stand the bedroom any longer. His wife kept a goat in it. The smell was awful. "Why don't you open the windows?" his friend suggested. "Nay, lad," was the reply, "if I did that all my pigeons would get out".

Two old ladies who lived at an isolated farm near Giggleswick worked when it was light and went to bed when it was growing dark. The exception was on a moonlit night when, if they had a cow in a receptive condition, they were known to take it to the nearest farm with a bull and have it served without the farmer or his family knowing anything about it.

When the old ladies retired to Settle—and they might be seen walking through town in clogs and with sacking as aprons over their working togs—they still went to bed, feather beds, with brass bedheads, by the light of candles or paraffin lamps. Their first job on moving into town was to have the electricity supply taken out. "It's dangerous," said one of them.

Feather beds were often used for the storage of money. The odd bedhead found itself used for blocking a gap in a drystone wall. In the days of big families, and limited money, up to half a dozen children could be fitted into bed, sleeping "top to tail", under newspaper.

Hannah Hauxwell, the daleswoman who features on the back cover of this book, has never been a good getter-up and, as she told my wife and I when we visited her at her dalehead farm in Baldersdale, "I'm afraid I'm not improving".

On the other hand, when a fell farmer whose nearest town was Hawes decided to go to London, and stayed at a huge hotel, he didn't lig in bed too long and, as usual, was up and about at 3.30 a.m.

Not being able to find a slopstone [stone sink] he went down several flights of stairs, looking for the kitchen. A member of the night staff told him of that jug of water and basin in the bedroom—the items of crockery I mentioned earlier.

Said the staff member, helpfully: "You can use that for washing".

The farmer replied: "Nay, lad, I've supped that".

Bible

IT'S AN old Yorkshire boast that there are more acres in Old Yorkshire (3,923,359) than letters in the Bible (3,566,840).

The Bible was used for devotions, for the recording of family births, marriages and deaths (in some handsomeley bound family Bibles, space was provided at the front for this purpose) and, in the case of a dog fancier, because he named his puppies after the numerous Kings of Judah.

At Boynton, near Bridlington, the Bible rests on a wooden lectern which is in the shape of a turkey, one of the Boynton family having sailed to Newfoundland with Cabot and being credited with bringing the first turkey back to England.

Bibical names for people were commonplace. An ancestor of mine was called Hobadiah (being usually referred to as Our 'ob). He was a farmer, with a practical outlook and no special religious affinities.

A small boy on the Yorkshire Wolds did not look for religious truths when he was told the story of Jacob and the Angels. Why, O why, were the angels ascending and descending a ladder? The boy, from a farm background, could think of only one reason: "'Appen they were in t'moult".

A vicar who read to the juniors the words "And they were astonished at His doctrine" invited the class of country children to explain what was meant, one boy saying: "They were fair capped".

The Wensleydale man who took up reading late in life impressed his wife with his progress. She told a neighbour: "He's getten through t'Bible now—and he's well on wi' t'*Darlington and Stockton Times*".

Kit Calvert, of Hawes, translated sections of the New Testament into Wensleydale dialect. When someone suggested that it was not seemly, he replied: "Christ spoke in a dialect". (When one devout Methodist was told of someone who read his Bible in Greek, he retorted: "English was good enough for St Paul, and it's good enough for me").

Here's an extract from Kit's translation of St Luke's account of The Nativity: ". . . an' t'was a lad, her first, an' she lapped him in a barrie cooat an' laid him in a manger, for ther' was neea room fer 'em i' t'ludgin' hoose".

Kit's father and some relatives worked in the Burtersett quarries. So did the old quarryman about whom John Thwaite, the Wensleydale dialect writer, wrote in verse:

They say thoo's iognerent, let 'em say,
Let 'em read ther' Bible an' then,
They'll finnd 'at oor Lord Hizsel caa'd oot,
Some unlarned an' ignerent men . . .

Taking the Bible literally was common in Dales congregations. As the parson read the 23rd Psalm, with its reference to "green pastures", a farmer whispered to his wife: "If they're owt like ours, they'd bide a bit o' good muck".

Chapel

YORKSHIRE is "fair littered" with chapels, which were once packed to the doors and are now thinly attended. The village chapel was simple in style, like a box with a steeply-pitched roof and a porch stuck on the front to cheat the weather. Sometimes, a chapel was built on a slope, leaving room for a chapel-keeper's house beneath the chapel itself.

At Barden, in Wharfedale, my father was taking a service when the chapel-keeper, a lady, said: "Cut thee sermon short when thou smells t'Yorkshire pudding". He did—and they sat down to a perfectly cooked Sunday dinner.

Inside a Dales chapel all was plain, even bare, with varnished pews, each with an umbrella stand and a row of chapel hat pegs. (It was said of an inquisitive person that he or she's eyes stood out like "chapil hat-pegs" or organ stops).

Many a chapel had to make do with a harmonium, which stood in fretworked splendour and wheezed its way through the hymns. A minister described the harmonium as "an ill wind that nobody blows any good".

One harmoniumist was addressed by a visiting preacher, who said: "I can't bring t'tune to mind. Doesn't ta think we can have a more up-to-date one?" She replied: "Nay—tha can't have it more up-to-date than this. I'm makkin' it up as I goes on..."

Another's contribution to the service came to an abrupt halt during the singing of "Fight the Good Fight..." The lady who was presiding at the harmonium said, with verbal economy: "Fight's ower. Cord's brokken".

The Yorkshire towns and cities had chapels which were mill-like in scale and appearance, except that the windows were rounded at the top. One of these gargantuan places of worship became a second home to one of two Bradford brothers who were scrap merchants. The other brother said: "Our Fred's a different man since he was converted by t'Methodists. He's happy and helpful to others. Then, sighing, he added: "I'd like to be converted, and be happy, but if that happened—who'd weigh t'scrap?"

Chapel folk are friendly folk. A Congregationalist in the West Riding was planned to preach at a city chapel and, being relatively new to the work, decided to save time by first shaking hands with the folk he saw waiting outside the chapel. When this task was almost completed, he suddenly realised he had shaken hands with a bus queue.

The rural preachers included dull men, such as one who was said to be "over-tired to go to sleep". Others got "het up" when "proclaiming the Truth". At the time of the 1914-18 war, as German hordes were reported to be crossing France, a biassed preacher was so worked up that he shouted: "Skiddadle 'em, Lord, skiddadle 'em".

Methodists do not believe in middle-men. They like to take their anxieties, fears, hopes and aspirations straight to the top. A preacher, at the time for prayer, invoked God to send down his only Son to save the assembly. At this point, one of the brethren exclaimed: "Nay, God—cum down thisell. It's noan a lad's job!"

A Wolds preacher who was particularly demonstrative in the confines of the pulpit waved his arms, raised his voice and occasionally brought a fist down on to the rostrum with a resounding thwack. A small girl said to her mother: "What shall we do if he gets out?"

Now and again, a preacher left the pulpit and acted out part of the sermon, such as the return of the Prodigal Son. The preacher went to a window, shaded his eyes against an imaginary sun and said: "By gum, lass, t'lad's comin' home agean. Kill t'fatted calf". He returned to the pulpit and confirmed that the lad returned from a far country, where he had been feeding swine. "And so he came home agean," said the preacher, "and he wor all clouted up wi' pig muck!"

Methodists in rural places tended to run their own affairs, for the minister had a dozen or more chapels to tend. A Steward welcomed a visiting preacher and often said a few prayers in the vestry before taking the preacher to the pulpit. One, having welcomed a woman preacher, prayed: "O Lord, bless thine 'Andmaiden who's come amongst us toneet. May she be amongst us as the right nail 'itten squarely on the head".

Methodist ministers were judged largely on their inclination to visit members of the flock during the week. A visiting parson gave words of comfort to a dying man. He was pleased to note that this man was not afraid to meet his Maker. From the deathbed came a weak voice: "I'm nooan feared of 'im. It's t'other chap I don't want to meet".

A Methodist minister was "touched" when he was invited to

attend a well-known Anglican, now laid on "a bed of sickness". He chatted with the old man, prayed with the old man, and then asked the wife why he had been called to the bedside. "Nay", she replied, "we're not sure what my husband's getten. We didn't want to risk t'vicar".

Let James R Gregson have the last words about a bad life:

If thou wants to play Hell, it's no good having a referee!

and

Talk o' t'Devil an' yer'll hear his clogs clattering.

Children

A LEEDS child wanted to know what sort of cloud God stands on. The child provided a hint, saying: "It must be a hard one". To the dalesfolk of old, a baby was "it" until the sex of the child was evident in the clothes worn. Babies make funny noises. A Dales farmer's wife said her grandson "balls [shouts] like a Friesian calf".

A Dales farmer's son is not very old when he develops positive views about livestock. One, at Hellifield, was so wearied when his father "haggled" for half an hour over the price of a cow he had brought that he said: "Get the begger sell'd".

At Bolton Abbey, a small girl asked her mother: "Did the monks build this place?" Mother replied: "Yes, love". The child remarked: "Didn't they leave it untidy?"

An attendant at the Great Yorkshire Show in Harrogate asked a little girl if she was lost. She replied, tearfully: "No—but me mudder is".

Food is a prime topic among the young, especially the fancy sort served up at parties. Children have to be sharp to get a share of the most tasty items, for as one girl said: "If there's ivver owt good, there's nivver nowt left".

Children can be brave and not cry, even when an accident befalls them. One who came limping home had a special reason for not crying. She said, forlornly, "there was nobody about to hear me".

Church

ANGLICAN Churches, being ancient, tend to have a foisty smell except where local women on the rota devote several hours a week to cleaning and polishing.

At Whitby, you must not camp in the Churchyard, which would not occur to most visitors, especially those of a nervous disposition. Hubberholme, at the head of Wharfedale, has an abundance of mice—wooden mice, the trademark of Robert Thompson of Kilburn. He adorned many a Yorkshire church with fine woodwork.

York Minster, at the heart of the county, was visited by two textile men from the West Riding. One stared in wonder at the enormous building. "What's ta thinking about?" said his friend. "Nay, nowt much. I were just trying to work out how many looms I could get into a place like this".

At Thornhill, near Dewsbury—which has a historic church—preparations were being made for the harvest festival. A lady was fastening a bunch of grapes round the neck of the brass eagle which serves as lectern when a voice rang from the back of the church: "Nay, lass, be careful, or thou'll throttle t'paycock".

Some of the Dales Churches, such as Kirkby Malham and Grinton, are like mini-cathedrals. Grinton has had some notable choirs and Robert Gill, of Reeth, used to say: "This lot could sing out o' t'*Darlington and Stockton Times*".

Churches tend to have prominent pews—one is so big it has its own fireplace—and a farmer's son, visiting an upper Dales church, confused them with something seen on the farm. He told his mother he'd seen "a lot o' booses [divisions between cattle stalls]".

When a vicar expressed his pleasure that a well-known toper should have turned up to the Sunday service, having slipped into a back pew, he said: "Oh, that's where I got to. I mun tell t'wife".

Not as many tales were told about Anglicans as Methodists, but Eleanor Winthrop Young (daughter of Slingsby, the mountaineer, who lived at Carleton near Skipton) recalled being taken into a local cottage when an argument was taking place between two young people. Eventually, the old father, a pillar of the Church, rose from his seat by the fire and said: "If prayer book's reet, its reet. If not—clap it at back of t'fire".

At one Yorkshire village lived two Dr Smith's—a doctor of medicine and a doctor of divinity. When someone asked where Dr Smith lived, a local man asked: "Who do you mean—'im at practises or 'im at preaches?"

Clothes

EACH of the villages of the North-East coast had its own style of hand-knitted gansey [jersey] and it was said that if the body of a fisherman was lifted from the sea, a local person knew the place of origin.

It was traditional to hand down clothes in a family until they were in tatters. A Moors child said to an inquiring friend: "No, I'm not Sylvia. I'm just Sylvia's dress". What had been heavy duty clothing was cut up into strips for making a pegged rug.

There is not much material in modern fashions. An old dialect writer noticed the beginning of a trend towards sparse clothing:

Bud noo all t'young lasses gangs fleein' aboot,
Wi' 'ardly eneuf on ti mak' a dish-cloot.

And a dalesman who saw a girl wearing a mini-skirt was heard to remark: "Yon skirt looks like a pelmet".

Coal For Nowt

TO YORKSHIRE folk, it's coil, not coal (or cowl, as they used to say in London). A miner in the Barnsley or Wakefield area got a ton of free coal a month. It was for a long time delivered by horse and tip-up cart.

The quality varied and the best coal went to the officials. Ordinary colliers had to mak do with second-class stuff. Some of them sold coal, knowing they'd get into trouble if they were caught. It was worth the risk.

With so much coal, some families kept one or even two fires going all the time. The house had a permanent heat haze. The last thing at night, someone banked up the fire. Next morning it was broddled (attacked with the poker) and stirred into glowing life. In a miner's home, there were always clothes hanging up to dry. The sulphury smell pervaded the whole house.

A miner who had been married for only three weeks had his first row with the wife when she let the fire go out!

I have never actually been to a miner's home where coal was kept in the bath. Early this century, there was no bathroom. When Colliery houses were built with this amenity, it tended to be put at ground floor level—and, remember, with a ton of free coal a month, there was something of a storage problem.

Courtship

IF YOU decide to go courting on Ilkley Moor, wear a hat or you might catch thi death o' cowld. The most famous courtship took place on the Moor in Victorian times. The young lady was called Mary Jane. We do not know the Christian names of the man.

The year was 1886. A West Riding church choir had a summer picnic on the Moor and a couple slipped away, engrossed in their happiness, to go courting. The man was baht 'at [without a hat] and the possible awful consequences were outlined, spontaneously, by members of the choir, singing to an old hymn tune called "Cranbrook".

In reality, a Yorkshire courtship usually lasted for two to three years. In one case, a couple had been "walking out" for 14 years when the young woman said to the man: "Isn't it about time we got wed?" He replied: "Who'd hev us?"

Many a courtship began when a young man plucked up courage to ask a girl he fancied for the last dance at some social event. This entitled him to ask if he could walk her home. A lad unwittingly asked a farmer's daughter who lived five miles away. He shrugged his shoulders and they began the long walk.

After a mile, he asked her for a kiss, and she agreed. He was so small, however, he dragged an old wooden tub from the side of the road, stood on it and had his kiss. A mile further on, he asked for another kiss, but was refused. The doleful suitor remarked: "Oh well, I suppose I can chuck this owd tub away".

Courting time was limited to a couple of evenings a week. One winter evening, a farm man was seen setting off with a paraffin lamp. He said he was going courting. "Nay", said the farmer, "I didn't need a lamp when I were walking out wi' a lass". "'Appen not," said the lad, "but see what thou got!"

Courtship could be sweet and marriage sour. A Pickering lad who was fond of telling his friends he was going to marry the best-tempered girl in Yorkshire changed his mind after the ceremony when she gave him a flinty look and said: "Now I'll unravel thee".

Cricket

YORKSHIREMEN are daft about cricket. Trevor Bailey, the great Essex all-rounder, wrote: "To them, it has become rather more serious than a mere game. It is almost a religion".

Yorkshire took pride in selecting native-born cricketers for its county side. As a Yorkshire spectactor said to a Lancashire spectator at a Roses match: "We play nobbut home-reared men. Ye'll play owt". He cheerfully ignored the fact that Lord Hawke was a celebrated exception, having been born outside the bounds of Yorkshire.

Once, when Neville Cardus watched Yorkshire play, the crowd roared "ow's 'at?" Involuntarily, he expressed a contrary opinion. A typical Yorkshireman eyed him from boots to crown and then said, slowly, "and what's the matter wi' thee?"

At Bramhall Lane, Sheffield, two Essex men were resisting the efforts of the home bowlers for hours. A doleful Yorkshire spectator said: "I'd rather fish in a pool where theer's no fish na watch them two bat".

An eccentric game is made even more so by the match which takes place on Boxing Day, regardless of the weather. You'd think the cricketers, in their "whites", would be cryptically coloured, but in fact the day is usually quite springlike.

Organised by the Northern Cricket Society, it takes place in the vicinity of Leeds. The first of the series was in 1949 and the first Society team was captained by Maurice Leyland.

A signpost near Beverley is inscribed: "Hutton 1". At about the time of the retirement of the immortal Len Hutton, someone scrawled on the signpost: "Not out".

Apart from the matches at Headingley and other first-class grounds, cricket can be indulged in wherever two or three enthusiasts are available. At a Moorland railway station, the stationmaster and porter took it in turn to bat. One day, a passenger caught the ball. The stationmaster was declared out.

The porter whispered to the stranger: "Thanks—he's bin in for a couple o' months".

When Vic Wilson took his benefit at Sheffield in 1958, he was batting when it was announced that a collection taken for him on the previous day raised £268. Wilson acknowledged the generosity of cricketgoers by raising his hat, whereupon a wag in the crowd yelled: "Now he's going round wi' 'is 'at".

Todmorden's border status (Yorkshire/Lancashire) is well-known. It was once said that if someone clouted a cricket ball for six, 10 to 1 it would land in Lancashire!

Dancing

YORKSHIRE has some dance specialities, including the sword dance, a variant of which is associated with Flamborough. In the Dales, old-time dancing is still popular.

Dalesfolk danced wherever there was room—where they would not become leg-locked. At Douk Ghyll, in Craven, a cart cover was stretched across the barn doors to cut down the draught. Harry Wilson and his Band wore topcoats and mittens throughout.

At Muker, dances took place in a room above a stable near "The Farmer's Arms". The dance room was flavoured by the smell of horses. Kit Graham's Band, in North Craven, used a handcart to transport a piano to the villages.

For a "village hop" in Craven, a rough wooden floor was strewn with flakes from a packet of *Lux* to make it slippery. "During the first few dances, we were all sneezing our heads off".

Tosside, between Ribblesdale and Bowland, is "an amazing place. . . it's out on a blooming hilltop, miles from anywhere, yet t'dances allus go off well".

Harry Cockerill, who played at Tosside and many another village hall in the Dales, was self-taught and perfected his technique with the accordion at High Greenfield, a solitary farm on the old packhorse road from Wharfedale to Horton-in-Ribblesdale. He was one and a-half miles from the nearest neighbour, so nobody complained of the noise.

No one wastes much time drinking and eating. The catering organisation is slick. You know when supper is imminent when a "Friendly Waltz" is played. As the last strains die away, doors and hatches are open, women appear with trays or tables holding plates of food, and in minutes everyone has a sandwich clenched in the teeth.

Will Pritchard emerged from the supper room at Austwick parish hall at a dance to see a young couple sitting out while Beresford's Band played some lively strains. Said Will: "Tha wants to git up and shak thi supper down".

Today, any number of "oldie" dancers continue to attend despite having had replacement knees or hips. A middle-aged man asked his partner in an old-fashioned waltz if she could reverse.

"Why, are you getting dizzy?" she asked.

"Nay," he replied, "you're unscrewing my wooden leg".

Death

TWO long-lost friends were delighted to meet up with each other again. One said: "I thowt you were deeard". The other said: "So I am. It's just that I'm too idle to stiffen".

The undertaker who had not had any "trade" for weeks said, dolefully: "Of course, I don't want anybody to die—but I've got to live". Perhaps he was the undertaker who married the midwife and used as an advertising slogan: "You can't escape us".

As two friends parted after being at the local mill, one said to the other: "Hes ta getten any red paint?" "Aye, and if thou pops round after tea I'll gie thee it". The other man went to the house after tea to be informed: "Fred's just died". "Ay, I'm reight sorry to hear that," said the visitor, adding: "Did he say owt about a tin o' red paint?"

The old custom of displaying the dear-departed in his/her coffin for a day or two before the funeral is not as common as it was. One neighbour, looking at the waxen features of her friend's late husband, and trying to find something cheerful to say, observed: "He's smiling". The newly widowed women retorted: "Aye—he doesn't knaw he's deeard yet".

Dentistry

IN CLAPHAM parish, children never complained of toothache. They knew that if they had aching teeth, their parents would get the local blacksmith to pull it out. An old chap recalls: "Once he got thee on a horse-hair sofa, wi' his knee in your chest, you'd no chance to escape".

Dentistry doesn't hurt any more, or so it is thought. A girl went to the dentist and, on her return, said to her mother: "You said it'd be painless. . .you should have heard him shout when I bit 'im".

The dentist who drilled a tooth for what seemed like hours looked puzzled and remarked: "Have you had this tooth filled before? I keep getting flecks of gold on the end of my drill". The old chap in the seat remarked: "Tha's takken so long, thou must have reached t'back stud o' mi shirt".

An ancient Swaledale man was persuaded to visit the dentist for the first time. He was asked which tooth gave him pain and replied: "First thou comes to". The dentist asked him to open his mouth. There was only one tooth left".

Dialect

IN YORKSHIRE, you don't earn—you addle. When you begin a job, you've "got agate". If you are going backwards, the Yorkshire expression of "back'ards-road" will give it extra expression. Untypically, it provides a longer version of the word.

If you've eaten till your fit to burst, you're "brussen". Those berries you have just picked are not blackberries but "bummel-kites". To be pleased is to be "chuffed" and if you're slack-set-up you've lost your sense of purpose.

Yorkshire dialect is rooted in the speech of the Anglian settlers, who were the first English. Their "nan-beautan" became the indispensable "nobbut". The Norse-Irish folk who occupied the upper dales were the first to laik [play] and use a stee [ladder]. If it rains, its "teeming" (if it isn't chucking it down!).

The Victorian dialect writers like John Hartley amused their generation with such pearls as "Ahr Mary's Bonnet":

Es-ta seen ahr Mary's bonnet?
It's a stunner an' nooa mistak!
Yoller ribbons, yoller rooases,
An' a gurt big feather dahn t'back;
Ah Mary went ter chu'ch last Sunda:
T'congregation did nowt but stare;
T'parson says, "This is nut a flahr-show,
But a house of prayer";
Ahr Mary says: "Thy 'eead's bald,
Nowt in it, ner nowt on it:
Would-ta like a feather aht o' t'back o' my bonnet?"

I have been using Yorkshire dialect to flavour the stories. A Milltown lad who spoke dialect was asked, during a religious education class at school, the name of the Biblical character who built an Ark. Crestfallen, the lad simply replied: "Noa". He was given full marks.

A Ripon boy who was travelling by bus with his mother, looked up the river as they crossed a bridge and said: "Look, mum. There's a waterfall". She corrected him with the words: "Weir, dear". He delightedly said: "Ower theer".

The Barnsley lass who said "booter" instead of butter was corrected until she began to pronounce the word correctly. She then asked the teacher: "What do I say for jam?"

Doctors

THE old-time dalesman didn't want to bother t'doctor unless it was summat serious, like dying. He'd try everything, including a dose or two of sheep medicine, before wasting t'doctor's time and chucking brass about, for until the coming of the National Health Service one paid for treatment.

The doctor with a large rural round had a horse, trap and often a driver (who might be grandly known as the coachman).

Today's doctors have cars, often car radios. They may summon an ambulance or even a helicopter.

The treatment they mete out is not necessarily out of a textbook. A locum in a large Dales practice met an elderly woman who hobbled into the surgery, leaning heavily on a stick. "We must do something about that bad leg of yours," he said, and turning to the receptionist he asked her to find a saw.

There was a rusty saw in the cellar. The doctor accepted it without a murmur. He advanced on the old lady; he took the stick from her hand and sawed off several inches, replacing the ferrule and saying: "You should walk better now".

The young doctor at a North Riding cottage hospital asked a garrulous woman patient to open her mouth. He slipped a thermometer under her tongue and told her not to speak for three minutes. The husband stared in amazement and said: "How much do them things cost?"

The old farmer had not been for a medical examination for many years. He was congratulated, but replied: "Nay, doctor, I'm often poorly but I say nowt. Every time I tell t'wife I feel poorly, she maks me stop smoking".

Some Yorkshire Speyks

IN PLAYS by James R Gregson:

He'll simmer quietly now he's letten t'lid off!

Ah can read him better nor big print.

Also:

She's that finnicky, she looks for lice in bald 'eeards [heads].

Of a poverty-stricken upbringing: I've licked a cleaan thible [porridge spoon] monny a time.

Overheard in Church

SCHOOLGIRL, all eyes as sidesmen take up the collection: "Our side's winning".

A Colne Valley preacher, at the conclusion of a sermon: ". . . that's what I think, though I knaw St Paul's agin me".

Father of a boy child, replying to a mid-Wharfedale vicar who queried the choice of "Homer" as a Christian name: "It's obvious. . . I keeps pigeons".

Bradfordian, watching Methodist ministers leave a city chapel after a synod: "I reckon parsons is like good muck—best spread out".

A small boy, impressed by the parade of a surpliced choir through a Wolds Church: "Look, mum—they're all going to get their hair cut".

Doggy Days

A VISITOR to one of the Dales farms where "open days" are held was impressed by the height of the nearest fell. "I bet you've been up there hundreds of times," he said. The farmer replied: "Nay—but dog has."

The collie dog is the Artful Dodger of the Yorkshire skyline. Without it, farmers could not run sheep on the "tops" for there would be no handy way of rounding up the sheep for seasonal jobs like dipping and clipping or in an emergency, such as the onset of a blizzard.

Faithful dogs are kept in retirement until life becomes too much for them and they are "taken to t'vet". Some dogs simply pass away in their sleep.

At Hawes auction, this snatch of conversation was heard:

"Did t'dog dee?"

"Aye".

"Poor do".

"Aye".

End of conversation.

Drink

SOME Yorkshire folk like it hot and some like it cold. In North Ribblesdale: "I like tea as hot as Hell and black as t'fireback". Of some poor tea, it was said: "Is t'tea begrudged or t'watter bewitched?"

At Barnsley, a man drank a pint of beer so quickly that a visitor to the inn could only stare with admiration. The drinker said: "Me throat were that dry, a pint 'ud nobbut wet one side. In any case, I've allus supped it like that since my accident". "What accident?" "A terrible accident—somebody knocked my pint over".

When a lad's mother was told her son had been seen "supping

whisky", she was concerned and asked: "Was it neat?" The informant, looking extra grave, said: "No—it were broad dayleet".

A lady who was dissatisfied with the quality of milk supplied by a local farmer went to the farm one morning with two white jugs and said: "Put milk in one an' watter in t'other—I'll mix mi own".

A waitress forgot to leave a spoon with the cup of tea. The customer said (sarcastically) that the tea was so hot he couldn't bear to stir it with his finger. The waitress took it away and returned with another, saying: "I think you'll find this is a bit cooler".

Electricity

TWO old ladies, living close to each other in a Wharfedale village were bemused as they emerged from the paraffin age into the bright new world of electricity. One complained that the electrician had "put t'leets in lile bottles and I can neither turn 'em down or blow 'em out".

The other, captivated by the continuing brightness of a bulb in her living room, said to a friend: "Doesn't it last a long time?"

Epitaph

Here lies (I will not write "asleep",
Because no bed is six foot deep
Beneath a pounded gravel heap)...
(Anon)

Fish and Chips

THESE are best eaten out of the paper, in the open air, on a frosty winter night. Fish and chips provide instant warmth (at times lifting the skin from the lips). The only discomfort is when a mixture of warm cooking fat and vinegar oozes between the fingers from a laceration in the greaseproof paper.

At Skipton, in the old days, a fish and chip shop used to be situated at Mill Bridge, beside the Springs Canal. So many pieces of paper were discarded over the bridge that on the following morning the dominant smell for anyone walking along the towpath was—vinegar.

An enlightened headmaster at Upton, near Pontefract, provided good facilities for children to have food at school. Naturally, he took into account their food—fish and chips. Twice a week, two monitors toured the classrooms and took orders, at the same time collecting the money. At 11.30 they went off to the shop with a large clothes basket, returning with the fish and chips, plus a bottle of vinegar and some salt which had been provided free of charge.

It is said that a man went into a Skipton fish and chip shop and asked for "Fish and chips—twice". Said the man behind the counter: "I heard you first time".

Food

IT IS related in Yorkshire, in favour of a good meal, that "it 'ods [holds] thee back up". The first Yorkshire Pudding is said to have been made by Angels. The Devil must have had a hand in some of the Yorkshire pastry I've tasted. James Gregson's aunt made such cloggy pastry "thou could shoe horses wi' it".

Until recent times, going to a restaurant was an extravagance for most Yorkshire families. To visit a cafe was a treat. A Leeds man who "went out" for a meal asked for beans on toast, tea and a kind word. The first items were served. He said: "What about the kind word?" Said the waiter: "Don't eat them beans".

(Moments later, the waiter dropped a tray. In this age of way-out sounds, under the guise of music, two couples got up to dance).

A Yorkshire saying runs: "Ta mich of owt is good for nowt". An

Eskdale man agrees. He does not like trifle because: "There's over-many tastes".

The men working on a large East Riding farm knew when the farmer's wife was making jam roly poly pudding for dinner. She only wore one stocking. The navvy who was lodging in a Dales cottage was asked by the householder if he fancied an egg to eat for tea. Said the navvy: "Aye, lass—and I'm that hungry I could eat t'ruddy hen that laid it".

The frail old lady who boarded a bus with a basket asked the driver to go carefully and drop her off at the hospital. When she was alighting, he asked: "Are you sure you're all right?" She replied: "Right enough. But I wasn't thinking of myself. I have a jelly in my basket and when I left home it hadn't quite set".

A Hawes farm man, visiting a local cafe in the old days, was handed the menu and said: "Yes". The same man, offered "beans on toast" said: "Aw reight—if thou hesn't any plates".

A girl from the village who was recruited to help serve a special dinner at the big house was told not to spill anything. "Don't worry," she said. "The family gossip is safe with me".

A Wolds farmer who was told by his doctor to have a simpler diet said: "Aw'm nut gooing to starve mysen to death for t'sake o' living a few years longer".

Funerals

IN THE old days (i.e., pre-1960), you always knew when a funeral was to take place. Curtains were drawn in the street or neighbourhood. People talked in whispers. The mourners were clad in crow-black clothes and even the townsfolk who had no knowledge of "the dear departed" showed their respect by standing still, the men removing their hats, as the cortege passed by.

The hearse was driven at a steady 10 miles an hour. Nowadays, it is driven as fast as traffic permits. "At Joe's funeral, t'driver was in that much of a hurry he left t'other cars behind. Joe had never travelled so fast when he was living".

At the Church—where, 10 to 1, the organist was playing Handel's *Largo*—mourners gave their names or business cards to the representative of the Press, who (up to the 1930s) also copied down the messages and names on floral tributes, such as "We'll miss you, dad" or "You'll always be in our thoughts—Amy and Bessie".

Generally speaking, if someone dies old in years and wisdom, a Yorkshire funeral is a happier event than a wedding. People tend to cry at weddings. At the funeral of a veteran they take the retrospective view—and chuckle. The spirit of the "dear departed" surely chuckles with them.

Yorkshire has innumerable funeral stories. "If thou doesn't laugh, there's nowt left for it but to cry". Perhaps this harks back to the time of early industrialisation when, in the insanitary boom towns, which evolved around the mills, the human lifespan was brief.

A "proper" funeral, with a church service, wreaths and a ham tea, is the prelude to giving the deceased a degree of immortality through an inscription on a gravestone. "It's summat folk can see".

At the funeral, the parson emphasises the finer aspects of the dead person's life. So does the average inscription on the gravestone, which has been described as "fair and false".

A cemetery testimonial looks on the brighter side of human character. What the visitors recall about the interred is another matter. "He wor a tight owd begger", says someone of the late lamented George. And that was a compliment in Old Yorkshire where no one was inclined to throw good "brass" about.

"Look at John Willie's stone. It says RESTING. He nivver did owt else".

But I've strayed away from funerals. At the funeral, everybody knew the departed very well and everybody seems to have seen him/her within a short time of death, for (as related) it was the custom to display the dead in an open coffin, usually in the bedroom but sometimes in the parlour, for friends and relatives to see.

"He looked weal, did t'owd lad. Aye, I reckon that holiday in Scarborough did him good".

The constricted modern house is not suited to putting the body on display in a coffin, especially in the spare bedroom. A daleswoman who visited her son, wife and their young children in a new Council house at Skipton was determined to find summat wrang wi' it, and remarked: "How's ta going to get t'coffin down yon steps?"

When the coffin of the former (formidable) wife of a farmer of the North East Moors was being borne with difficulty down the stairs from the bedroom, it was jolted, a sound was heard inside the coffin and they found the wife was not dead after all.

She lived for several more years, bossing the family without mercy, and once again she appeared to die. Once again, the coffin was carried down the stairs from the bedroom.

As the bearers went down, step by step, the anxious husband said: "Go easy, lads".

A tale is told of a bearer moving swiftly down a flight of stairs with an out-of-control coffin slithering behind him.

A funeral is a time for fulsome tributes. Methodist ministers tend to go "over the top" in their tributes, so much so that the elderly widow of a Dales farmer not noted for his benevolence towards his fellow man grew restive and said to her son: "Thou'd better go and look in t'coffin. I think they've getten t'wrang chap".

A Bradford man wanted to be buried just inside the churchyard "so I can be first out on t'Day o' Resurrection".

Near Barnsley, a new grave ran from north to south. The gravedigger referred to the difficulty he had in fitting it in and said: "He'll have to have an extra turn on t'Last Day".

A funeral might be a time for business, such as that small matter of how much Fred wants for "them half-bred yows".

For the old, the committal at the churchyard is a time for some joy.

Said an 86-year-old: "You've no idea how grand I feel when I walk out of a kirkyard". Someone remarked to a 94-year-old with mock severity: "There's not much point in thee going home, is there?"

The funeral service is followed by a good tea, wi' nowt spared. York hams are world famous. Cooked ham, thinly sliced, is the most common funeral-tea food—with lettuce, etc—and if you went to the Co-op in the old days you could claim your divvy both on the funeral and the tea. Ham was the staple food for funeral teas but "Our Ethel wor buried wi' chicken".

The cemetery was the place for a person to be seen on a sunny Sunday, for it was then that local families went for a walk among the bones of their ancestors. It was also a place for courting couples during the early phase when a boy and girl were content merely to link arms.

A shy suitor took his girl to a grave and said that was where his grandparents were buried. He showed her the next grave, which was "where mi mum and dad were buried". They moved on a yard or two and he remarked: "Ay, lass, that's where I'd like us to be buried".

It was the nearest thing she got to a proposal.

Nowadays, cremation is the thing. It is not uncommon for the ashes of the "dear departed" to be kept on the mantelpiece for a while until the next-of-kin decide where they should be spread. One woman is reported to have said: "I keep thinking I'll put some of 'em in an egg-timer. He didn't do so much work when he was here; so he might as well do some work when he's gone".

A spinster at Huddersfield told a neighbour, on the day a mutual friend was about to attend the cremation of a third husband: "I can't get a man—an' she's got husbands to burn".

Disposing of the ashes lacks the solemnity and ceremonial of a "proper" funeral, with hymns like "Abide with Me" to clean out the tear ducts. Spreading the ashes is a lonely business, left to the survivor or to a good friend.

One lot of ashes was spread on Ilkley Moor. Instead of standing at a graveside, listening to the slurring of the coffin and to the intoning of a parson, there was just the whine of the gale and the momentary sight of a cloud of dust (a good man's earthly remains) travelling at 40 miles an hour over rock and heather.

Hens and Eggs

O B STOKES, a former Editor of *The Telegraph and Argus,* told me the story of a Bradford man, one of several local millionaires, who was so "tight wi' his brass", he employed his native instinct in making money by taking surplus eggs from his hens to sell to his mill operatives.

Those were the days when Bradford, its prosperity based on wool, was noted for the wealth of its inhabitants. It was said there were more Rolls Royce cars to be seen in Darley Street (known then as the Bond Street of Yorkshire) than in any other street in the country.

One morning, as the manufacturer-who-also-sold-eggs waited for his train on the village station, an egg rolled off the overful basket and cracked on the station platform.

Nothing daunted, he bent down and—with his morning newspaper—scooped up the yolk, to the astonishment of his fellow travellers.

"Nay", said one, "tha's noan going to eat that, aht ta?"

"Nivver thi mind," came the rejoinder, "it'll poach".

I don't know what many a poor Yorkshire family would have done without hens or, more precisely, hen eggs. A hen doesn't need a lot of space. I marvel at its patience, just sitting there, day in day out, producing eggs, with mini-jaunts to the beaten earth which used to be part of the landscape, here to preen and scratch and have a drink of water.

In days when people did not wander far from home, "dad" spent a lot of time "dahn at t'hen run", where he could have a quiet smoke, fettle [repair] the hut and set the dog on the rats.

When the years of egg-laying are over, a luckless hen has its neck wrung and is served up at the next major meal. It was the fate of one such to be killed and cooked against the visit of a Methodist minister after the morning service at Chapel. Later, during a tour of the farmyard, the minister admired the Rhode Island Red cockerel which stood on a post and crowed loudly.

The farmer, who had noticed the speed at which major portions of the chicken had slipped down the visitor's throat, said: "It should be proud; it's getten a son in t'Ministry".

Jimmy Gregson wrote of someone as having a neck "like a plucked chicken" and being "as flustered as a hen that wants to sit", which reminds me of the man who had lived all his long life in one Dales village but, being restive, was forever moving from one house or cottage to another.

The vicar asked if this gipsy-like existence had affected him in any way. "Nay, vicar," was the reply, "but it's made t'hens a bit nervous. When they hear a removal wagon, they jump up on their perches to have their legs tied".

Holidays

YORKSHIRE holidays really began in 1625, when a Mrs Farrow went to the fishing village of Scarborough—an attractive spot, with the ruins of a castle on the headland and some lovely countryside just inland in case the roke [sea-mist] came in.

Mrs Farrow was feeling out-of-sorts, as were many in that pre-penicillin, pre-aspro age. On one of her walks, she saw rust-coloured water bubbling up as a spring and after drinking some she bathed her aching feet.

She might have died and the world of tourism would never have heard of Mrs Farrow. Instead, the revolting liquid made her feel better. If a medicine was pleasant to take, it obviously wasn't doing you much good!

Mrs Farrer made an appointment with Dr Whittle, told him of her experiences and asked his opinion about the rust-coloured spring water. He agreed it must be beneficial. He began to prescribe it to his patients, making a bit o' brass in the process. The more gullible patients were told to drink 25 gallons of sea water, at a pint a time, over a period.

The next time he recommended total immersion in the sea, with a pint of sea water to follow. By 1740, sea bathing was popular. The women wore costumes that virtually covered them, and they operated from bathing huts on wheels so that they were away from the prying eyes of men.

The wells of Scarborough were commercialised and the place became a spa, or spaw, if you were posh. A bandstand was built by the wells in 1875. "Taking the waters at Scarborough" had an appeal that lasted just into the next century. By that time, the place had blossomed as a resort, complete with hotels, boarding houses, cruets, sand-castles with paper flags, donkeys and dancing.

Scarborough was by now just one of a string of coastal resorts that included Whitby, Filey and Bridlington. On the west coast were Blackpool and Morecambe ("Bradford-by-the-Sea"). Morecambe's shortcoming was its beach, which is a mixture of sand and mud. Years ago, newly-weds who went to Morecambe were fond of telling friends they had "honeymooned on the West Coast".

Those who did go on holiday took their pleasures seriously. A North Ribblesdale couple spent the first evening, Saturday, looking for a place of worship to attend on the following day. Their children groaned as the hours went by; they were anxious to make sand castles on the beach.

When Sunday dawned, and duty to God had been done, the small girl broached the matter of building sand castles, only to be told that it was not the sort of occupation to be undertaken on the Sabbath. She sighed and said: "Will it be all right if I make sand chapels?"

Wilfred Pickles told the story of the West Riding family who were staying in a boarding house at Blackpool. It was one of those multi-storied houses, with endless flights of stairs.

The family had assembled in the dining room when the small boy said: "Muuum!" From the way in which it was said, the mother knew he was about to ask to go to the lavatory and as this was not a seemly subject for a dining room she "shushed" the lad and whispered: "Slip upstairs".

Peace returned to the dining room. Then, from high up in the building, came a resounding voice: "Muuuuum!" She could not ignore it, and shouted: "What, luv?" There was silence for perhaps three seconds, then the lad shouted: "I can see t'Tower when I'm on t'closet!"

The Yorkshire coast is notable for its fossil beds. A man who found a fossil on the beach near Filey asked a local expert about it. He was told the fossil was 160 million years old and "as fossils go—it's nobbut a lad".

Horses

YORKSHIRE was renowned for its horses. Yorkshire horse dealers were well-known for their shady practices, not least theft. George Borrow wrote that if you shake a halter over a Yorkshireman's grave, he'll rise up and steal it.

The somewhat gruesome Victorian ballad, "Clapham Town End", deals with two Yorkshiremen and their desire to sell horses. The nag offered by one was dead; the other was ailing. In the end, they swapped. The dead horse having been skinned, its purchaser faired worse than the other man, who was better off "by a skin and four shoes".

At Yarm Fair, a man bought a horse from a gipsy and on the way home discovered he was half-a-crown short in his change. He returned to Yarm and confronted the gipsy, who said: "I'll not give you half a crown—but tak another nag instead".

A Swaledale farmer who regularly attended Brough Hill horse fair, near Kirkby Stephen, says that to get a bargain here a horsey man must have made every mistake in the book. The "travellers" were so adroit that one of them might buy a white horse in the morning and sell it back—now coloured black—to the same man in the afternoon!

If you could not afford to buy a horse, then you might hire one. A Moors man approached a farmer who, in calculating how much to charge, at so much a day, asked: "How long will you want it?" The hirer said: "As long as you've got; there's five on us".

Alas, some urban-based horses fared badly, being over-worked and under-fed. A visitor to the home of a mean-minded man remarked: "I see thou's gettin' a new hoss. . .for surely that's t'framework for one in t'hoss box".

In country as well as town, much depended on the ability of the horse to remember a routine. In town, milkmen rarely had to raise their voices. The horse knew when to start and where to stop.

It was the same with one horse on market day. It knew that it must never walk past an inn.

At yet another hostelry, the farmer went inside. Some lads took the horse from the shafts, put it back the wrong way round and harnessed it up as best they could. The inebriated farmer, emerging unsteadily from the pub, was heard to say: "I'd nivver have believed that a hoss could chuck a cart ower its heeard".

The great attraction at a Yorkshire gala was a parade in which Lady Godiva, wearing next to nowt, was riding a white horse. An old chap who did not normally attend the gala said he was determined not to miss this one, adding: "I can't remember when I last saw a white 'oss".

Few blacksmiths remain. A garageman who took over a smithy fancied himself as a shoer of horses, though his experience was almost non-existent. Sensing that he might be cheap, a local farmer allowed him to shoe a horse.

When he returned to collect it, he found the horse lying on the ground but wearing a splendid new set of shoes. "Tha's med a good job of t'shoeing, but hoss doesn't look so good," said the farmer. The mechanic agreed and, looking across at the workbench, added: "Hoss has bin like that since I took t'last foot out o' yon vice".

A Swaledale farmer who had a horse and cart regularly drew up outside the Tan Hill Inn to buy a whisky—for his horse. He would not buy one for himself, explaining: "It wouldn't be right. I'm driving".

If a horse became ill, a farmer did not rush to get a vet, who had a nasty habit of charging for his services. There were local remedies. One man said he had used paraffin, so his friend gave an ailing horse a liberal dose of the stuff. The horse died. When next he saw his friend, he mentioned this and added: "What 'appened to thy horse?" The farmer sighed and said: "It died—

same as thine!"

Inevitably, the time came when professional help was needed.

In the early days of veterinary science, a horse, which was lying, with closed eyes, had a blue pill dropped into its mouth. Minutes later, the pill having "worked", the horse stood up, bright-eyed, and cantered off across the large field.

Said the farmer: "Tha'd better give me two o' yon pills; I've got to catch the begger!"

Never bet on horses. "It's a fool's game," said a Malton man, who had been such a fool for years. "I put some brass on a horse t'other day and it came in last. I wouldn't have minded, but I should have noticed that t'jockey was carrying a thermos flask and some sandwiches".

Illness

IN YORKSHIRE, go by the colour of the face. Red means fresh sunburn or high blood-pressure. Pink is healthy. "Drip white" is distinctly unhealthy.

Those who are ill are said to be "off colour" or to have a "poor colour". Lethargic folk are "under t'weather". In the days before wonder-drugs ["tha wonders what's in 'em"] a person's condition "warsened".

Hopefully he/she would "tak a turn" and soon be "on his feet". Now and again, the decline was irreversible and the victim, if a man, "popped his clogs".

Yorkshire folk leave medical terms to t'doctors. The dalesman with a broken arm simply "had a wing up". Doctors used to have the assistance of a local woman who specialised in bringing babbies into t'world and laying-out anyone who had died. At a childbirth, she'd wipe her hands on a tea-towel and keep the husband busy by asking him to boil vast quantities of water.

(Wilfred Pickles told the story of a girl who asked her mother: "Where did I come from?" Providentially, they were in the garden, where mother was planting seeds. She held a tiny seed in the palm of one hand and told her daughter she began like that. The child was enchanted and replied: "Was my picture on the packet?")

Doctors, like vets, used to be expensive. One of the updale flockmasters told a visitor: "We don't have doctors up here; we dee naturally".

An old-time patient expected to be given "summat in a bottle". Such medicine was usually pink and pointless, except that it made the poorly person feel better. A doctor said to a Sheffield woman: "I hope your husband's taking his medicine religiously". She replied: "Sorry, doctor. He curses every time I give him some".

Carter Platts, the angling writer, who spent his last years at Skipton, used to say it was possible for the wind to be too strong for good sport. He received a note from a man who asked about local conditions as he was thinking of visiting Wharfedale for a few days of fishing.

Platts wired back: "Can't do much at present. Bothered with the wind". The angler replied: "Sorry to hear it, old man. Try gin and ginger—hot".

It is not unusual for a doctor with a huge rural round to "sound" a farmer's chest in the hayfield or, drawing up beside a village green, to blow the horn of his car "so the old ladies can come out and have their pill bottles re-filled".

Years ago, when Yorkshire folk were so less well informed about medical matters, a miner was told by his doctor that he must give up alcohol and asked: "Nay, lad. Can't I have an operation instead?"

And when two old dalesmen met in Leyburn market to discuss the serious ailment of a mutual friend, one said: "Ah reckon only a post-mortem will show what it is". "Aye," said the other, "but he's so weak now, he'd nivver stand one".

Married Life

Oh who is the man who is warst off i' life,
To be without wit or to hev a cross wife?
Baath of 'em are cases that's hard to surpass,
But he's in t'warst pickle that's dealt without brass.

(Tom Twistleton, North Ribblesdale poet).

WHEN A Brighouse couple had been married for 50 years, a reporter visited them to collect information for an article. He asked the old man: "To what do you attribute your long married life?"

He replied: "I decided that if there was a row brewing, I'd leave t'house by front door, walk round t'terrace and come back in at t'back door." The reporter suggested he had peace of mind. "Nay," said the man, "plenty of exercise and fresh air".

An old Wharfedale couple were fratching. The sound of the argument drifted into the street. The vicar entered their home to restore peace and said: "Just look at that dog and cat, lying peacefully side by side on the mat in front of the fire".

"Aye", said the man, breaking off his argument in mid-sentence, "but thee tie 'em togither and see what happens".

A Heckmondwike woman told a friend that her husband had stopped smoking after 40 years.

"I bet thou's pleased". "Aye".

"It'd tak some will-power".

"Aye, it did that—but I've plenty of it," said the wife.

Mean-mannered

SOME Yorkshire folk have a mean streak. They've experienced hard times. Brass hasn't come easy. "They hang on to what they've got". A few are lazy with it and "can nobbut fill a bed an' empty a cupboard".

When a Keighley man noted for his mean ways was seen scrapping paper off a wall, a neighbour naturally concluded he was going to re-decorate—at long last. "Nowt o' t'sooart," he replied. "We're flitting to another house".

A Dales meanie, during the 1939-45 war, had a thriving little "black market" trade in meat and collected it from farming friends and relatives in a small, battered, nondescript van. One evening, he was driving home when he was waved down by a policeman. The driver did not stop. His wife, who was sitting beside him, said: "Now they've got you! Yon policeman will have takken t'number of t'car".

The driver replied: "They'd have a job on. Afore I left home, I plastered it wi' cow muck".

At a farm in the Vale of York, a basket of apples was being topped up with the finest fruit so as to look well on display in York. The farmer said: "There's tricks in every trade. When my awd fadder made besoms, he always put t'shortest bits o' ling in t'middle".

The meanies are those who have something given and want some luck [a gratuity following a sale] with it. They think in terms of discounts, not tips, for services rendered. Many years ago, a farmer's son, reporting on a visit to London, shocked his relatives by confessing he had used a taxi—at 2s.9d.

He considered it was cheap. "I gave him three bob. He seemed to expect more. He looked me straight in t'eye and said I must live in Yorkshire. I looked him straight in t'eye and said I did—and could I have my thruppence change, please?"

Vicars and church treasurers have to be "tight wi' brass".

When a vicar caught a burglar red-handed, he asked him what he was looking for and was told: "Money". Said the Vicar: "Give me ten minutes to get dressed and I'll help you".

At Christmas, a boy ate one of the small silver coins which had been cooked in the pudding. They took him to the parson for, as his mother said: "Our vicar can get money out of anybody".

Of the layfolk, a story is told of a vendor of patent medicine, who was in town on market day, and attracted a crowd to his stall by squeezing oranges until he was holding just a dripless mush and bits of skin. His medicine was to build up a person's strength.

The vendor invited members of the crowd to squeeze oranges. If he could not squeeze another drop from a crushed orange, he would hand over £5.

A small chap stepped forward. He grasped an orange. The veins stood out on his brow as he squeezed. The orange went to mush but, with a super-human effort, he managed to coax out yet more juice.

The strong man tried, but the orange did not yield another drop, so he patted the little man on the back and said: "How did you manage to do that?" And the little chap replied: "I'm a church treasurer".

A man who hated mean or grumbling people told a crusty old villager he must "think on t'Israelites". He added: "They got stuck out in t'Wilderness for forty year. And it were all for growsing".

A door-to-door salesman was about to walk up the path to a South Yorkshire cottage when a neighbour told him not to waste his time, adding: "Ah reckon yon chap's that hard-faced, you could bend nails on it".

A mean sportsman was annoyed when he had acquired some rabbiting and had taken a friend to the area so that they might shoot some bunnies. After half an hour, the sportsman remarked: "We haven't hit owt yet. We'll just miss another two—and then call it a day!"

Midges

ONE of Nature's terror weapons, unleashed in Yorkshire hayfields and wherever in the countryside people find themselves when the weather goes still at "t'edge o' dark" [dusk], is the all-weather midge. By itself, it is laughably small, but this creature flies in khaki clouds.

John Thwaite, the Wensleydale dialect writer, had experience of being under attack by midges:

When t'midges land than t'neck yan wipes
An' [hay]reeaks er dropped an' fooak leet pipes.

Hoo [how] t'li'le beggars mak yan scrat,
Midges allis see te that!

Neea shakkin' off, neea good te pleean,
They help therselfs te fat an' lean.

T'owdest worker—sixty, mooar,
Nivver knew 'em wass [worse] afoor.

Miner's at Home

HERE'S the last verse of a sentimental Music Hall song entitled "The Miner's Dream of Home":

I saw the old homestead and faces I love,
I saw England's valleys and dells;
I listened with joy, as I did when a boy,
To the sound of the old village bells.
The log was burning brightly,
'Twas a night that should banish all sin,
For the bells were ringing the Old Year out,
And the New Year in.

It wasn't like that in a South Yorkshire colliery village, such as Hemsworth, Upton, Frickley, Grimethorpe and Long Row (this row had over 50 houses). The old Colliery owner was not exactly agin a pretty countryside—he liked to have some round his big house—but he didn't like to see landscape doing nowt but grow grass and feed a few cows.

If there was coal, then let's have it out and sell it! It was a process known to the Victorians and Edwardians as keeping t'brass moving. The medieval church and cottages with honeysuckle round the doors; the fields, hedges and copses didn't stand a chance if coil [coal] was located beneath the fair acres.

In a twinkling, Capitalism had created a Colliery village in all its ugliness, with pit, terraced houses, shops (including t'Co-op, of course), a school for 300 kids, steam locos drawing lines of rattling wagons—and t'slagheap rising immediately beyond the houses to blot out half the sky.

But what about the miner's home? Let's visit a redbrick, blue-slated, muck-enveloped colliery house in a village near Pontefract as it was early this century. If it was one of the "new" villages, and the Yorkshire folk—with their "ayes" and "e bah gums"—had, as neighbours, families from Wales, Scotland and the North-East, where work was scarce but coal so common it could be picked up on the seashore.

Life in a Colliery village was all to do with status—Colliery owner, vicar, doctor, manager, overman, deputy and then the grey mass of miners, who spent much of their time coughing up coal dust.

Each was accommodated not according to his deserts but to his social position. The ordinary miner, with a permanent heap of low-quality coal at the back door, and his house backing on to another to save brass and space, was creating the wealth but had to manage t'best he could. Needless to say, every miner was a paid-up member of the new Labour Party.

The Yorkshire miner's dream of home took in a house where he was more aware of what was missing than of what he had got—no attics, no cellars, no kitchen and no bathroom. The living room was too small to swing the proverbial cat.

With so much free coal to use, the fire glowed, day and night, giving the family the impression of living in a kiln at a brickworks. Anyone entering the house was aware of the all-pervading sulphury smell from working clothes hung up to dry.

The first job in a morning was to broddle, or apply the poker to a fire that had been backed-up with "slack" late on the previous evening. The man went to work; his poor, thin-faced wife continued her war against dirt in the over-crowded living room, and the front room with the sofa and two easy chairs (only the better class folk had a piano, a book case and an aspidistra in a pot by the window). The house had a kitchen and two good bedrooms, each with a chair and cracked lino.

The housewife contrived to have a hot meal ready for her man the moment he entered the house, even though, at the end of the week, he might have decided to spend an hour or so at the club on the way home, by which time his food would be dried up and tasteless.

He bathed, which is a posh word for sitting in a zinc bath in front of that white-hot coal fire while his wife or one of the kids scrubbed his coal-smeared back. The zinc bath was slipped back on its hook in the tiny backyard where stood the only closet [now known poshly as the toilet] and ash-bin. The night-soil men from t'Council made their rounds to clean them out. Next morning, the housewives splashed pink disinfectant all over the street.

Happily, conditions improved. The newer Colliery villages were better places. Baths were installed at the pithead. The Yorkshire miner's dream of home was no longer a nightmare. The Music Hall miner heard "the bells ringing the Old Year out and the New Year in". At the mining villages where families from the North East had settled, you'd also hear (at a minute to midnight) the clatter of dustbin lids as the last of the Old Year muck was laid to rest.

Money

A YORKSHIREMAN likes to make brass, but he isn't usually showy with it. Exceptions were the West Riding textile barons, including Alderman Joseph Denby, of Keighley. Asked if his large Yorkshire estate was difficult to manage, he replied: "Nay, but sometimes t'lads leave t'gate oppen—an' let t'deer out".

A South Yorkshire miner, who lived in a terrace house, enjoyed the wealth of the local aristocracy by going to the gates of a huge park on Sunday morning and looking through the gates at miles of parkland, with big trees.

One morning, the aristocrat rode up and said: "What are you doing, my good man?" The miner said: "I'm just looking at my estate". "It's mine," boomed the aristocrat. "Well," said the miner, "all tha can do is look at it. And that's what I'm doing. So it's as good as mine".

The owner, amused, said: "Have you a big estate?" "Oh aye, tha mun come round and have a look at it". The aristocrat arrived in the mean street of terrace houses and was led into a small yard with brick walls and a tin bath hanging from a nail. There was the diminutive outside closet and a wash-house.

The visitor said: "You're estate is not very big". The miner looked at the sky and remarked: "But see how high it is!"

A Skipton man said: "Nivver marry a woman wi' brass. Mine had five pund when I wed her—and I'se never heard t'last on it". A successful Wensleydale farmer went to Hawes market with his pockets full of sovereigns, which meant he had to wear his heavy-duty galluses [braces].

Eventually, his pockets became threadbare and his wife suggested that she might carry the money in her handbag. He said: "Nay, lass—mend me breeches. Thou can lose thee handbag. I'se nut likely to lose mi breeks".

Those were the days before paper money became common. A Pickering man who was given a 10s note with his change was worried about it. He met an old friend, a solicitor, in the street and asked: "Is this note reight?" The solicitor peered at it, said "yes"—and gave the farmer 7s.6d change.

In the days when a good wage for an ordinary worker was rather more than £1 a week, a Halifax man shocked his neighbours when he said he had sold a whippet for £1,000. You could have bought a terrace of houses with that amount of money. A friend queried the sum. He said: "Well, I didn't really spend owt. I traded yon whippet for two £500 cats".

Money was stuff to be saved. A suitor took his girl friend to the cinema and paid sixpence each for seats, the cheapest available. They were at the front, where benches rather than tip-up seats were to be found. The girl had neckache from peering upwards at the huge images on the screen.

When she told her father what had happened, he was so indignant he said she must go right round to his house and give him sixpence. She did. He said: "Nay, lass, thou shouldn't have bothered".

As his lady-love turned to go, he added: "Thou could have browt sixpence in t'morning".

The Dales farmer had worked hard and long and had accumulated a lot of money. A friend said to him: "Thi nephew's just waiting for thee to die—and he'll soon spend t'lot". The farmer remarked: "If yon lad gits half as much satisfaction out of spending it, as I had making it, he'll do varra weal".

Bradford woolmen were often pleading poverty—though few of

their workers believed them. One of them defined a woolman as "a bloke who buys wool at £2 a pound, sells it at £1.80 a pound—and when his will's published you find he's left £750,000".

Brass attracts brass. As a poverty-stricken man lamented: "I reckon, t'chap 'at's born wi' a silver spoon in his gob finishes up wi' gold fillings in 'is teeth".

An old friend, Dr J D Pickup, told the story of George Wright, of Silsden, who eventually resided in the Workhouse at Skipton but returned to Silsden to attend the Sunday School Anniversary at the Methodist Chapel.

Someone had approached George at the Workhouse and asked him if he could borrow a shilling. George had replied: "Ah've only one shilling as ah can lend out, and if tha can get it back, tha can borrow it". The other man asked who had the shilling. George said, triumphantly: "Thou has!"

Motoring

TRAMS, then buses, were the forms of transport used by ordinary folk. In Old Huddersfield, a bus conductor rang the bell and said to a man who had just boarded the bus: "Na then, 'od tight—or thou'll wish thou hed done!"

Yorkshire had its several motor manufacturers, including Jowett Cars, of Idle, Bradford, who made a mark in the 1920s. The firm was set up by William and Ben Jowett, who decided on a small car as opposed to the petrol-guzzlers with which they competed. With a Yorkshire craftiness and humour, they advertised their six horse-power car as a "seven" and claimed it passed the "seventeen" (as made by others) "like a seventy".

An early advertisement included a photograph of a Jowett standing before an old monastic building. The registration number of the car was C99. The information was "leaked" that the number referred to No. 99 in *Hymns Ancient and Modern*—a hymn which begins: "Ride on, ride on in Majesty".

Years before the Jowetts roared out on to the road, the pioneering motorists had needed a sense of adventure. They clattered along to far-off places like Grassington or Helmsley. Sometimes people succeeded in getting to the seaside and back in the day.

In the earliest period of holiday motoring, it was not unknown for a driver to have to reverse up Sutton Bank near Thirsk or Buckhaw Brow near Settle, using the lowest possible gear.

Garages were few but occupied strategic positions, such as Clapham, where Mr Barton (agent of Ingleborough Estate) set up business, with hand-operated petrol pumps. The owner of a large car stopped for fuel but left the car engine running. The perspiring man at the pumps eventually said: "Do you mind cutting the engine, sir? You're gaining on me!"

Elsewhere, the driver of a Rolls Royce who was not far from home stopped for a gallon of petrol. The pumpsman said: "What's ta do? Is ta still weaning it?" An old lady calling at an East Yorkshire garage was astonished to see petrol being pumped from a bowser into the earth; she thought the process was the other way round!

Moorland roads are not the places for overtaking. There's the odd bend or dip. Now and again a ford may be encountered, as between Low Row (Swaledale) and Langthwaite (Arkengarthdale).

A motorist who was in a hurry on this highway (in a literal sense) risked overtaking a car which was travelling at a moderate speed. When he saw the other motorist later in the day, he remonstrated with him for not allowing him to pass.

"Nay," was the reply, "I didn't knaw tha was in a hurry. Tha were going at about t'same speed as me".

Another road hazard on the high Pennines or north-east Moors is provided by footloose sheep. I have had to brake on seeing sheep licking salt from the road at Buttertubs, between Hawes and

Muker, and have uttered unkind words when catching up with a flock in a narrow stretch of road.

If the sheep are going in the same direction as the car, the motorist can only grind along and hope they will soon be turned into a field. One day, an impatient motorist grew weary of the confusion which was being created as two men and three dogs fought a battle for dominance over a hundred sheep. The motorist wound down a window of the car and addressed the nearest man, asking: "Who is the master of this flock?"

The reply was unexpected: "That little black-faced 'un at t'front".

Music

NEDDY DICK (Richard Alderson), of Keld, in Swaledale, kept in his cottage a battered harmonium, a stand holding over a score of bells taken from old grandfather clocks and—the pride and wonder of the upper dale—a "rock band" composed of "musical" stones collected from local becks.

Apart from Neddy's use of ancient stones, Yorkshire's musical history might be said to have begun with the song of Caedmon at Whitby. A monument records that he was "The Father of English Sacred Song" who "fell asleep hard by, 680".

Halifax has Yorkshire's oldest choral society. The local people prefer their music live. A man who listened to a concert on one of the early radios was heard to say: "I've nivver liked tinned meat and I'm blowed if I care for tinned music".

Huddersfield's Choral Society is noted for its performances of *The Messiah*, which is also rendered (never given) at any other place of worship capable of raising a choir. A Yorkshire chapel choir, rehearsing for the annual performance of *Messiah*, was not pleasing the conductor with their singing of "For Unto Us a Child is Born".

Said the conductor: "Please could I have a bit more reverence—and not quite so much astonishment?"

Edward Elgar, a distinguished musical visitor to Sheffield and Leeds, entrained for Giggleswick in the 1880s and stayed with his friend Dr Charles William Buck. The two young bachelors also played Chamber Music in a fug of tobacco smoke.

Oh—how they smoked! Buck alone had 50 tobacco pipes and clouded the air to such an extent that a special sliding panel in the living room door could be moved to expose a hole through which the smoke might pass and disperse.

Elgar's early letters were full of fun. A brief note from the *Queen's Hotel* in Leeds accompanied a ticket for Buck. Elgar added: "Behave decent and don't smoke during the musick".

Old Age

HENRY JENKINS, who died "a very aged and poore man" at Ellerton-on-Swale, December 9, 1670, and was interred at Bolton, was reputedly 169 years old.

Edmund Bogg, author of many Yorkshire books, repeated an unlikely tale of a visit by a Richmond attorney to Ellerton-on-Swale, where he approached a feeble white-haired man, thinking it was Henry. The man heard him out and then said: "Ah dean't know owt aboot it! Gang yer ways in t'hoose and ask me fayther, he'll appen tell you".

The attorney entered the cottage and saw, seated in the inglenook, a shrivelled and helpless wreck of a man, who said his fadder was at t'back o't house, chopping wood and would tell him about it.

The attorney moved on and found the "patriarch" looking fitter than his grandson. "He listened courteously to what the lawyer had to say and related happenings which had occurred 150 years earlier".

He were that mucky he'd drop i' bits if thou took a scrubbing brush to 'im.

Yorkshire longevity led to a couple attending the funeral of a son who had died aged 60. The father said to his wife: "Ay, lass—I telled thee we wadn't rear 'im". They had lost a daughter a few years before and now, of their family of three, "there's nobbut yan on 'em wick now".

On his 90th birthday, a Swaledale man said: "I'm a lot better on mi legs than I was 90 year ago".

Old folk who are mentally alert may have "gone off their legs" and be confined to bed or an armchair. One old man said to his daughter, who was about to go shopping: "If thou's going near t'cemetery, pop in and git me another pair o' legs".

Quakers

AT SCHOOL in West Yorkshire, a boy defined a Quaker as someone who "nivver grumbles, nivver wants to feight and nivver answers back. . .Me dad's a Quaker. But not me mum".

A Quaker who heard a strange sound during the night presumed there was a burglar in the place. He must, of course, not resort to violence, yet he picked up a shotgun, located the burglar, pointed the gun at him and said: "I wouldst remove thyself, Friend, for I am about to shoot in the precise spot where thou standeth".

Railways

A YORK man who found, when he made his first rail trip, that he did not care for this means of travel, cheated the railway company by buying a return ticket—and walking back.

Heard by the Settle-Carlisle: "When owt happened to a steam loco it allus managed to twine itself to t'next signal box. If a diesel loco decides to lay doon, it lays doon where it is. You've lost 'im".

Salvation Army

A SALVATION Army band played a lively medley of hymns in a West Riding town. One man went round with a collecting plate. A spinster woman placed in it a ten shilling note. The man, overcome by her generosity, said: "Thanks, luv—you can have any hymn you like". The woman said: "I'll have him wi' t'big drum".

A lady Salvationist went up to a woman who had been listening to the band playing "At the End of Our Journey We Shall Wear a Crown" and asked if she would like to wear a crown. "Nay, lass," was the reply. "I'd look daft wi' a crown on mi head. I'll stick to mi owd bonnet".

School

GARDENING was a popular subject at a village school. A new boy was seen crying and the teacher asked a friend what the matter was, only to be told: "He's dug a hole and he wants to take it into school".

Of a teacher who kept the children hard at their lessons: "By— she did put us through t'small sieve".

A teacher drew the letter S on the blackboard and asked a boy what it was. He said: "A door sneck".

Seaside

AN OLD chap who lived at Appersett, near Hawes, told me he hadn't seen the sea. He did not want to see the sea, adding: "It's nobbut watter". An old friend says: "It's just a horizontal line, with water below and clouds above".

When walking along one of the pier extensions at Whitby, in a gale, I met an old salt and we sheltered for a while, listening to the whine of the wind and the boom of waves against masonry and the nearby cliffs. I found the conditions terrifying. The old salt said: "We're having a bit of a blow!"

The old chap from Ripon who was persuaded to go to Scarborough for a week's holiday (his first real holiday) was provided with some fancy pyjamas by his son, who said: "Wear these at night". The old man protested: "Nay, I nivver go anywhere at night—nobbut bed".

In the early 1930s, a time of Slump, a West Riding family, by much scrimping and saving, managed to get enough money together for a holiday in Bridlington. They had such a good time that as the "brass" began to run out, mother said: "Eh—if only we'd pawned some of your grandfather's stuff, we could have stayed here for another week".

Two Whitby fishermen, meeting at a local inn, were in a boastful mood. As time went by, the stories became more imaginative. When one man spoke of a record catch of fish, the other tried to impress by telling of the day he caught half a dozen jellyfish.

"What's special about that?"

"Nay", said the boastful fisherman, "each jellyfish had a different flavour".

A schoolteacher in the Pontefract area who, many years ago, took a group of boys to Staithes, on the Yorkshire coast, for a week's camp, first accompanied them to the pawn-brokers to be kitted out, and then they entrained for Staithes.

No boy had been on the train before and certainly not to the seaside. Teachers off duty would go down to the *Cod and Lobster*, near the sea, with the headmaster, and partake of refreshments. At 10 p.m. the drinkers would briefly leave the inn, and the landlord would come out with some fish and give it to the policeman, who would depart. The customers returned to the bar and stayed until the early hours, when the headmaster was carried back to camp.

Sheep

THERE are sheep—and sheep. Those in the upper dales are lile horned sheep with hard, tight fleeces. The farmers do not leave them alone for long. When they have been on the fell for a short time, they are gathered to be brought down for one of the many annual jobs, such as tupping, dipping, lambing, spaining [separation of yows from lambs] and clipping. The sheep are handled so often, it's a wonder they don't get mange.

Years ago, there was enough brass to employ shepherds. They did not like their employers to interfere with the management of the flock, least of all the selection of a good tup. If anyone else picked an animal, they were determined not to say anything good about it.

"Nay, boss," said one of them, to the farmer who had been to the sales and returned with a new tup, "tha says yon tup has a pedigree". He paused, looked at it intently and then pronounced on it: "Well—I've nivver sin a sheep more in need o' one".

The lad employed on a big sheep farm did not show much aptitude in working with collie dog and sheep. One day, he did rather better and the farmer said: "I'm glad to see you used your head". His reply: "I used my blinkin' feet".

Counting sheep is a special skill. Many different methods are used, but the commonest is to count in two's as the sheep pass through a confined space, such as a gateway.

I took a retired North Craven farmer to Gargrave Show and, impressed by the large attendance, I asked him how many people he thought were to be found in the field. "I don't know," said the farmer. "But if tha gets 'em to run through yon gate-hole, I'll soon tell you".

An Eskdale farm man had three attempts at counting the moorland sheep. His figures were 92, 89 and 88. The farmer sighed and said: "Well, we're on t'reet side. There should nobbut be 85".

When sheep are heavy with wool, they are prone to rigging or kisting [turning on their backs and being unable to right themselves]. At Barden, in Wharfedale, I was told: "If you see a yow [female sheep] kisted, ye mun upskuttle it [turn it over]".

Sheep may be overblown with snow when there is a blizzard. They are usually clustered under snow at the lee side of a wall, where the farmer uses a dog to scent them out before digging down. A Wensleydale farmer, asked by a holidaymaker how he found sheep which had been buried in snow, replied: "I've fun 'em all sorts o' ways—sometimes deeard".

The old shepherd was not pleased when he was told he was going to have a lady assistant. "T'last time I heard of a woman doing this job, she made a mess of it," he said. The farmer asked who this woman was. Said the shepherd: "They called her Bo-Peep".

Shopping

THE Bradford grocer, asked for some toilet soap, said: "Do you want it scented". The shopper said: "Nay, lad, I think I can manage to carry it". (Perhaps it was the same customer who said a neighbour was "that thin he's like an owporth o' sooap on washing day").

At the village stores, a customer asked the owner if he sold paraffin. He nodded his head. She mentioned firelighters. He nodded his head. "Well, then," said the customer, "wash your hands and get me two ounces of ham".

The shopkeeper was proud of the amount of work done by his wife; he remarked to a friend he wished he had two or three more like her!

Seen in a West Riding shop:

"The Lord helps those who help themselves but the Lord help those caught helping themselves here".

The Thrifty Ones

"DEW as they dew i' Dent; if tha's neea bacca [tobacco], chew bent [grass]".

Of a careful grocer: "He's that mean, he'd nip a currant i' two".

A dying dalesman whose last request was for an ounce of baccy was told by his wife: "If thou's bahn to dee, awf an ounce'll be plenty".

Time

THE boy's wristlet watch had stopped. He took it to the repairer, who opened the back and deftly removed a dead fly. The boy sighed with relief. "No wonder it's stopped—t'driver's dead!"

Transport

"DOES this bus go to Halifax".

"Aye". "It says Brighouse on t'front".

"It says INDIA on t'tyres, but we're not going theer".

Visitors

DALES farmer to camper: "Tha's nivver gaen to lig under yon' lump o' clout. . ." (Ella Pontefract).

Walking

CLEVELAND in the clay; take two boots, bring one away. (Traditional).

A party of ramblers were described in Wharfedale as "reight predestinations".

Father urged the flagging family by saying: "We've nobbut ten miles to go—and that's only two and a-half miles each".

When some walkers complained of the length of the lane to a Moorland farm, the farmer replied: "If it was any shorter, it wadn't reach".

A walker who asked for directions from a farm to the village was told: "Go ower yon stile, through yon wood, then ask again. I've bin no further than that missen".

Weather

WE'RE even proud of Yorkshire weather. There's so much of it—seventy inches of rain a year at Ribblehead, t'biggest snowdrifts on the high Pennines and, on the coast, summer roke [sea mist] so thick, you can taste it. As I heard at Whitby: "T'roke was that thick 'at if we hadn't knawn where we were, then we wouldn't have known where we were".

In the presence of visitors [such as those from America, Germany and Lancashire] we're inclined to brag about the weather.

At Haworth—where, if you've read your Bronte, the wind "wuthers"—an American was telling about the extremes of weather at home: about violent winds, lightning, thunder, hail and snow. Then it was the Yorkshireman's turn. "'Appen you do get such weather—but at Haworth we can hev it in t'space o' twenty minutes".

In some parts of Yorkshire, plants have a struggle to live. Up on the moors, they have to keep their heads down. But down in tropical Yorkshire—about Selby—it's so growy they've to prune all the telegraph poles.

"Aye", said one native to another, "when it rains tha can fair here stuff growing; it's enough to make stuff jump out of t'ground. The other man paled as he said: "By gum, I hope not. I've three wives down in t'cemetery".

Modern weather forecasters have their eyes stuck on computer screens. It would do them—and us—good if they went outside now and again, and looked at t'sky.

Dales farmers are good at forecasting. Some of them use a barometer, though as one remarked: "I reckon nowt tiv it cos it's as changeable as t'weather itsen". Another, despairing when the barometer showed "fair" for days on end, took it out into the rain and said: "Sitha!"

A barometer is not much more effective when used on humans. A Wolds farmer's wife told the doctor she put t'barometer on her ailing husband's chest. All it registered was "wet and windy".

Some Dales forecasts are not easy to understand. A farmer forecast: "It'll happen donk and dozzle a bit and mebbe a flister or two, but there'll be nae gret pells". Another, someone doleful, said: "I reckon it'll be a mild winter this coming summer". If there's a red sky at night, then the shepherds (what few of them remain) are delighted. A small boy, camping with the Scouts near Ingleborough, looked at a red sky and said: "It's bin so damp to-day, t'sky's gone rusty".

In a drought, the vicar is asked to pray for rain. One man remarked: "I will if you insist, but I don't think we'll have any while the wind is in the present quarter". Another refused, saying: "Not while the roof is off the vicarage". It's not just the vicar's prayers that matter. When an old lady was offered a seat on the bus for an outing—it was the only seat, which had become vacant because someone fell ill—she remarked: "I don't know if I should tak it.

You see, I've already prayed for rain".

With the weather, try to look on the bright side of things. "Nice morning?" said a visitor to Skipton. "Aye," remarked a doleful local man, adding "and thou gits thi share on it". A man living on the Plain of York at the time of the 1914-18 war asked a visiting parson about the war news. The parson brought him up-to-date. The man absorbed the information and then, trying to look on the bright side of things, added: "Well, they've getten a fine day for it".

The Weather Clerk is inconsiderate. A Wolds roadman of old was digging through a snowdrift. He grunted: "Why can't t'snow and frost come in summer, when t'weather's decent?"

Weddings

THE vicar, officiating at a wedding, asked a young bridegroom, who lived at a dalehead farm, if he would take the woman to be his lawful wedded wife. The lad replied: "I come on purpose".

The editor of a Yorkshire newspaper wrote the report of his own wedding and decided to have a break from routine. So instead of describing the bride's wedding dress he described what he had been wearing: "The groom had donned a blueish business suit, recently cleaned and pressed. Beneath the coat and waistcoat was a freshly laundered white shirt, across which lay a grey and blue tie".

A middle-aged bridegroom was having second thoughts about his bride-to-be. His best man whispered: "Sarves thi reight. Tha's bin round t'orchard and finished up wi' a crab apple".

Wireless

FRIENDS of a Pennine farmer suggested he might replace his battered old radio. "Nay," he replied, "it's takken me twenty year to git used to t'folk on this 'un".

Women

Wi' a Yorksher mother 'til y'er twenty-yan,
An' a Yorksher lass fer a wife, lad, than:
Wi' brass in t'bank, an' a weel-stocked farm,
Noo Ah've fun' oot 'at yan taks lile harm.

(John Thwaite).

Work

LIFE was all bed and work, thought the South Yorkshire miner, as he prepared to leave the horse for the pit. He was only half awake as he tried to slip on his clogs. His wife said: "Nay, lad, tha's trying to put 'em on t'wrang feet". He sighed and said: "I knaws that—they should be on thine".

Mill workers were penalised for being late. One of them, approaching his workplace, was met by the boss, who said: "Hooter's gone". Said the millman: "Nivver—they'll pinch owt these days". He was seen setting of for home at mid-afternoon. He told the boss: "I were late this morning and I'se not bound to be late in t'afternoon as well".

The man who landed a job as night watchman after some years of unemployment thought his wife would be pleased at the news. She said: "What a waste. I've just got thi some new pyjamas".

A farmer usually had hired help, providing bed, board and a bit o' brass. A Wharfedale farm labourer remarked: "My boss doesn't spoil me wi" brass—but I work accordin'." Women were expected to do a hard day's work, and in Dentdale one said, as her long working life drew to a close: "I'se done owt and everything".

Rousing a worker in a morning was often a difficult job. A farmer knocked on the hired man's door and urged him to get up. From the room a voice demanded: "Is it raining?" "No". "Is it snawing?" "No". "Is it foggy?" "No". "Well then—I'se not feeling so well".

The man who could not sleep, with the result that his work was suffering from his tired condition, was urged to paint the bedroom window of his cottage black. He did so. He awoke, wondrously refreshed, but saw that he was late for work. He rushed down to the farm, apologised and heard the farmer say: "That's aw reight. But where was tha yesterda' and t'day afore that?"

Sometimes there's no work available, as in South Yorkshire between the wars, where the old dialect work laik [play] was frequently used by the unemployed. An American couple, travelling northwards through England on holiday, stopped near Barnsley and asked the way to the "Lake District". A grim-faced miner told them: "Tha's arrived".

At school, a teacher was re-telling the Biblical story of Christ calming the water on the lake. She asked: "What is a lake?" A miner's son said: "When me dad don't go down t'pit".

There's no end to work. A visitor to Whitby asked a man what he did outside the holiday season. He said: "Same as in summer—but with an overcoat on".

A little old lady in Bridlington asked a police constable if he could see her across a busy road, "Hold on, love," he replied, "I'll just pop across and have a look".

Yorkshireness

"NIVVER ask any man thou meets i' Yorksher if he's from Yorkshire. If he is, he'll soon tell thee. If he isn't, then why embarrass him?"

A Few More Speyks

OF a small joint of meat: "When I got it cooked, it wor just like another crack in t'meat dish".

Of an awkward chap: He's a bit bad to shave.

She's as miserable as sin. When she talks to anybody she says nowt.

No one nivver yet 'eard on a duck sending its young 'uns to college to learn to quack.

She's aboot as nimmle [nimble] as a steean pig-trough.

Folk are losing their own common sense through listening to t'experts contradicting one another.

Ivverybody knaws ivverybody else, or somebody else 'at does.

She's war ner a hen fer pickin' stuff up.

And Some Yorkshire Graffiti . . .

ON a farmer's Land Rover, parked in the market town: "Don't wash me—plant summat".

On a grimy dairy van in the West Riding: "This model is also supplied in white".

Ee Ba Gum!

A VISITOR to a West Riding town heard two girls talking and thought they were speaking Chinese. One said: "Whowashiwi?" (Who was she with?) and the reply was: "Shewawiahsue" (She was in the company of my sister Susan).

Basic Yorkshire

Addle. To earn. It is the Yorkshireman's special joy to addle lots o' brass [money]. He likes to mak it, even if somebody else has the pleasure of spending it.

Agate. Nothing to do with the familiar wooden structure with five bars and hinges. If you've got agate, you've started a job. Some people never end a job; they're always agate or "on the go".

Amang-hands. If you want a job doing, go to the busiest person you know; he or she will be able to slip it into a busy work schedule, thereby doing it "amang-hands".

Anent. Was the favourite word of a lady in the Wakefield area. It means against. She lived anent t'Co-op.

'Appen. It means "perhaps" but is also a useful continuity word in a boring conversation. (See also "Aye").

Avver-breead. More properly haverbread, which is rolled-out oatcake—the type of oatcake your Grannie made using a "bakstun". She draped the oatcakes over a rack near the fire and as they dried they looked like wash-leathers.

Aye. The word to use when you want to keep up your end of the conversation without really trying. Just remember to change the inflection of your voice each time you use it. And at least look interested in what t'other chap's saying.

Backend. The period towards the end of the year. The word is derived from the Danish "bagende", which means the hind part.

Bahn. This is for the Yorkshireman/woman on the move—bahn ta wark, bahn 'ome or just "I'se bahn" [going to t'toilet].

Baht. It means "without", and became world famous through a song about an incautious, hatless lad who went courting Mary Jane on Ilkla' Moor. He went baht 'at [without his hat].

Belk. This signifies a rude noise (belch). The belch does at least avoid a boke (retch).

Bethowt. It's all to do with remembrance. An old chap will say: "Ah just bethowt missen".

Brass. No prizes for this one. It relates to money—the stuff to addle. "They" do say that brass talks; it allus says "goodbye" to me.

Brazzen. Usually applied to a hussy [a very common woman], it signifies that she has no sense of shame.

Brek. To break. Tha might "brek it i' tu"' (break it into two). Then it's well and truly brokken, which is the fate of some of your children's new toys on Christmas morning.

Brussen or Brossen. It really means "burst" but may also be used with regard to someone who has eaten far too much and is reaching the bursting stage. One Yorkshireman's response was to slap his full stomach and say: "Ay, good belly, Ah wish thou were empty agean". In the Dales, the word brossen may be applied to a nasty "gathering" on arm or leg which swells, then bursts—"it's brossen"—and will now mend up.

Bumblekites. An attractive word for blackberries, to gather which people fall into ditches, are lacerated by thorns, stung by insects—and then discover that the best bumblekites are just out of reach.

Caingy. It means what it sounds like—bad-tempered!

Cap. Not the object which some people use to fan their tea with but a word expressive of surprise. A Yorkshireman, astonished by something he has seen, says: "I were fair capped".

Caulkers. These were the irons at the bottom of clogs. The only drawback was that if the snow was deep and crisp and even, the "carkers" [Swaledale] became bunged up with clods of snow [known as coggers]. Boys loved to raise sparks from their caulkers by striking them against a hard surface like a pavement.

Cawfead. It relates to a silly man and is presumably derived from calf-head.

Champion. This applies to everything you like—brass bands, pork pies, your health and even that purple vase Aunt Edith gave you (the word being used only when Aunt Edith is in earshot). If you're feeling healthy and wealthy, then life's Champion.

Cheg. This word is all to do with chewing. Which reminds me of the Dales farmer who took his wife's false teeth with him when going off walling for the day. As he told a friend: "There's too much being chegged at our place between meals".

Chunter. You will have heard a chunterer—one who is ceaslessly complaining about summat or other. For, after all, in this modern world there's plenty to chunter about.

Clag. A word meaning "to stick". If you're clagged you've got something heavy in your mouth—some underbaked bread or a lump of cake which you are finding terribly hard to dispose of. A clag situation is eventually relieved by drinking.

Clarts. They are what they sound like—"cow claps" or, if you wish, bovine dung.

Clarty. From the previous item, you may guess that we are now concerned with a word for "mucky". Clarty applies to Dad's overalls, children's hands and field gateways. (why do they always put the gate in t'clartiest part of a field?).

Clemmd. Now we are on the subject of being thirsty. An old friend told me about her father and brother who were great walkers. "They always put a best foot forward when they saw a church tower or spire—for it was 10 to 1 there was a pub next to it".

Clout. It is a multi-purpose word concerned with (a) clothing, for you must not cast a clout till May is out; (b) with corporal punishment, once meted out to a small boy, and (c) with the hitting of some inanimate object, such as a cricket ball, out of the field.

Coit. The last thing to be donned over your ordinary clothes before leaving the house. (In the plural, sometimes confused with quoits).

Coop. A cart body on sleds, drawn by a horse, and once used widely on High Pennine farms.

Cowl-rake. Used not so much for cowl [coal] but for getting rid of embers. Also useful for hurling at the neighbour's yowling cat. In the Dales, a cowl-rake was for off-loading manure from a horse-drawn cart during the springtime routine of muck-spreading.

Crammly. Someone who is unsteady on his/her feet.

Daft. Applied to a silly person or circumstance, such as the stuff you are reading at this moment.

Docken. The name given to the plant called dock, the antidote to a nettle sting, two plants which a benign nature decreed should grow side by side.

Doff. To take off, being applied to caps in the presence of "betters" like the vicar, doctor and squire. You doff your cap when entering a church, also a house (unless you're forgetful) and when you see a funeral cortege passing.

Dollop. An ugly word, often applied to a heavy, shapeless lump like someone you don't like or a dumpling.

Dowly. A word summing up a miserable or lonely condition, being used when t'weather isn't up to much ("t'morning looks as though it's bin up aw neet"). Also applies to someone who is "under the weather" and hasn't said owt inspiring for t'last two hours.

Duffy. Hay which is dry and light enough to blaw away.

Eyt. For "eat", of course. A Yorkshireman/woman is not usually kysty [fastidious] about food, as long as it doesn't cost much, though he/she has some preferences, like fish and chips, followed by rice pudding (see "Clarty") and pieces of rich fruit cake (see Clag). Then it's off to sleep—till teatime.

Faff. This is when a person is trifling with something in an irritating way. Someone says: "Stop faffing about".

Fettle. To mend something—a gate, yon owd clock, our lad's bike, etc. May be used to mean cleaning up t'house.

Feyt. Means a fight. Early fights take place in playgrounds. Sometimes a little lad teases a big lad by saying: "Wanna feyt?" He actually made it sound like "One off Eight" and before the big lad was riled, he would shout the answer: "Seven".

Finnd. For "find", occurring in one of the old West Riding sayings: "It's a lot easier to finnd a fault than lose one".

Flay. Old Norse, meaning frightened. A farm lad up Ribblesdale way saw his first railway train and later told a friend: "It were fair flayed o' me, gave a low moan and buried itsen in t'grund".

Flummoxed. If you're "fair flummoxed" you're bewildered. Aren't we all in this messy age?

Fog. Not the meterological condition, half way between cloud and smog. In the farming world, fog also refers to the second flush of grass in a meadow, which is why you sometimes see an advertisement: "Good Fog for Sale".

Foisty. A name for fusty, the damp and smelly state attained by hymn books in an old and little used church. Also applies to biscuits which have not been kept in a tin.

Fotty. For some reason, many Yorkshire folk say fotty instead of forty. When you attain your fortieth birthday, it's best to start counting back.

Fowks. A nice homely word for people. "Eh, lass", says the husband as his wife returns from the Co-op with loads of groceries and gossip, "fowks'll say owt".

Frame. Used for someone who shows promise and has been told to "frame thissen". (An alternative is "shape thissen").

Fratch. To quarrel, of course. One old man found an answer to fratching. He said his little piece—and then, as his wife began to take, he removed his hearing aid.

Fun. In this case, meaning "found", as in the statement: "I fun a sixpenny bit dahn at t'allotment".

Gallowa. A sturdy type of pony used in the Dales. Named after the county in south-west Scotland. Packhorses moved goods along the old green lanes between England and Scotland for centuries before the transport revolution.

Gallowses. The Yorkshire word for braces, devised for "'odding thi trousers up".

Gaumless. A gawby is a fool and gaumless describes a foolish person. Of him it is said: "He's so gaumless, they can do nowt wi' 'im".

Gawp. To stare intently, the lower jaw drooping with astonishment.

Gert/gurt. A word meaning "big"—gurt hill, gurt fooil, etc.

Getten. What you've got!

Gezlin. A gosling, reared on a farm in the upper Dales, walked to the market town in autumn and sold to an arable man to be fattened on the stubbles for Christmas.

Gimmer. It's best to leave this (and associated sheep terms) to the flockmasters. Gimmer relates to a female sheep between the first and second shearings—a two-year-old, in fact. See what I mean?

Ginnel. This is a narrow alleyway between high walls. It was said of a Brighouse man that he was "so bow-legged, he couldn't stop a pig in a ginnel".

Gob. This is a word meaning mouth, or "cake 'oil". (Nationally, gobsmacked has taken over from the word dumbfounded).

Goose-gog. The local name for gooseberry. Mothers warned their children about eating too many or they might get bellyache. A Mother told an inquiring child that babies were found behind gooseberry bushes.

Gradely. A nice, comforting, pleasant, innocuous word meaning good, but not quite Champion.

Gripe. A fork used in the garden. Also the name of a type of water poured down the throats of babies who haven't "been" for ages.

Grund. For Mother Earth, against which drunkards are often found ligging.

Gumption. Or common sense. "That lad's short o' gumption".

Guts. A general reference to the intestinal tract and stomach. With heavy drinkers and those who eat too many goose-gogs, the guts tend to ache a lot.

Hands-turn. Used in the sense of helping. "Jack's bone idle; he nivver does a hands-turn".

Ivvery. A much-used word meaning "every". Ivvery time it's used, the writer's unsure whether to use one "v" or two.

Jock. A packed meal taken to mill or workshop. By one o'clock, a worker had etten his jock.

Kem. To comb. Applied by old-time farmers to the process of raking loose hay off the sides and back of a load of hay being taken some distance to the barn.

Kep. To catch owt, from a common cold to a Swardle tup.

Kitle. A lightweight working coat favoured by farmers, enabling them to feel dressed up among the muck.

Kitlin. A kitten, playful but not yet able to draw scratch patterns on your hands with its claws.

Kysty. For someone who is fastidious with regard to food. In the old days, when nearly everybody's stomach rumbled now and again with hunger, you ate all that was put before you. A farm man who tripped up when the dinner bell was sounded at a big farm said to another: "There's no point in rushing now. Food'll have all bin etten".

Laik. Old Norse word, meaning to play. You can laik with yon kitlin (see above) or laik football. You laiked if you were unemployed—"Nay, I wor laikin' aw last week".

Leet. To light a fire, a gas mantle or boiler (using a taper) or perhaps a bonfire. Natural light also counts—dayleet, moonleet, etc.

Lig. To lie down. "He wor liggin' in bed till tea-time". In the Dales, a liggin' grund is where peats are laid out to dry in the summer sunshine and breezes.

Lish. Relates to agility. Young 'uns are lish.

Lollicker. The luvly name for your tongue. It was rude to stick it out except when requested by Mum, who periodically felt your forehead ("E, Dad, our Charlie's running a temerature") and asked to see your lollicker. (Anything paler than pink led to you having a dose of Fennings Fever Cure or some Castor Oil. Ugh!).

Lop. Another word for flea (from the Scandinavian word "loppa"). In Yorkshire, a particularly lively person was described as being "as pert as a lop".

Lug. An ear, the word being derived from the "law" mark (applied to sheep ears by the Norse folk). A naughty boy had his "lug belted". Our Charlie (see "Lollocker") was frequently asked if he had washed behind his lugs.

Maffly. Also Mafflin and Dafflin. Mentally confused, sometimes temporarily, when a man had a wandering mind and said "I'se feelin's a bit maffly today", or permanently muddled, as occurs with some people in senility.

Malarkie. Larking around and getting into mischief when bored.

Mangle. The barbaric implement with wooden rollers used on wash-day for squeezing surplus water out of newly-washed garments. It also squeezed many a luckless child's fingers. The mangle was operated by a handle set on a wrought-iron wheel. At least one child, recruited to help with the mangling, found it helpful to sing a lively hymn, such as "Onward Christian Soldiers", while turning the wheel. It also ensured that the correct speed was attained.

Mash. An essential part of the tea-making process. Tea leaves are a herb and must be allowed to stand for a couple of minutes, when they are well and truly mashed. "Now they've putten t'tea in lile paper bags. It's not easy to open 'em and t'stuff inside's like powder", said one old lady. There's a woman in every Yorkshire street who'll tell you your fortune after looking at the old-fashioned tea leaves lying in the bottom of a well-drained cup.

Meyt. Sunday was the great day for meyt [meat]. Mum managed to get enough brass together to "buy a joint". There was some left to be served cold with mashed potatoes on Monday, and what was left then was minced up for Tuesday. Local dogs fratched over the bone.

Midden. The lile building at t'bottom of t'back yard wheer thou put t'asses [taken from under the coal fire]. Another sort of midden was a walled area outside a shippon which during the winter received all t'muck from cows—muck that was spread on t'fields in early spring.

Middlin'. Means "moderation" and applies to anyone who is just ticking over. "How's ta doin', lad?" "Nay—I'm middlin'." Sometimes the man's condition is slightly worse; then he's "nobbut middlin'."

Missus. An affectionate term used by a man for his wife. What she calls him, especially if he drops some beetroot on t'new carpet, is another matter.

Mizzle. A weather term, used for fine drizzle, known as "liquid sunshine" on the Pennines, where summers tend to be cool and cloudy.

Moan't. A useful word, meant "mustn't". You must have heard someone say: "Tha moan't do that".

Moithered. A state of being harrassed. Most young mothers are "moithered" nearly all of the time.

Mooinleet Flit. What used to happen if you lived in a big town and you hadn't enough money for the rent. You gathered your sparse belongings together on a cart and set off at night to start a new life where, hopefully, the cost of living was even cheaper.

Muck. An element in the process of making money in West Yorkshire. (See also "Clarty").

Muckment. Just rubbish. Everybody's got some muckment.

Near. Surprisingly, to non-Yorkshire folk, the word "near" can be applied to someone who is stingy [over-careful wi' their brass].

Nivver. It means "never", of course, as in "thou'll nivver master t'job". Nivver is also useful, as an interjection when someone is retailing gossip and you do not want to stop the flow of words.

Nobbut. A word frequently used for "only", as in "I've nobbut getten two quid left".

Nowt. Or nothing. Applied variously, as in "Tak nowt" or as a response, "That's nowt", when a person is trying to impress you.

Onny. For "any". There are lots of onny words, such as onny-bit-like [tolerable], onnygait [anyhow], onnywear [anywhere], onnyweal [I must be departing], onnyroad [at any rate], onnytime [at any time].

Owt. Or "anything", being just about the shortest effective

Yorkshire word. The standard business conversation runs as follows: "Owt?" "Nowt". "Mornin'." "Mornin'."

Parky. A word to describe chilly weather, when "thou mun lap thissen up" [don a warm coat].

Piggin. A lile bucket.

Pig-oil. Where they keeps pigs, of course. Grandfadder went to t'doctor wi' pains. Doctor said: "Where do you get 'em", so he could locate the seat of the trouble. Grandfadder replied: "In t'pig-oils". (That's where he had to bend almost double to clean t'pigs out).

Poke. A bag which features in one of the best-known Yorkshire axioms: "Nivver buy a pig in a poke". The translation: "It is better when buying something to see what you are about to purchase". The Yorkshire form is snappier.

Privy. An earth-closet, that little rose-embowered edifice at the bottom of the back yard. There are two holes on the seat in most closets but nowadays people in such a situation don't seem to like company. The toilet paper was last week's newspaper, cut into little squares, a job while listening to the radio play on Saturday night, or the family kept the tissue used to wrap oranges.

Puddins. The intestines of a pig.

Reeasty. Some foodstuffs which, in the pre-refrigerator age, had gone rancid.

Rowk. A state of untidiness. Also known as "being all of a scrow".

Scrat. From the Danish kratte, to scratch. Hens scrat in a run. Dad scrats when he fancies he's got another flea on his back. In the Dales, someone who never stops working is known as a scratter and a friend will say, wearily: "Is ta still scrattin'?"

Scurf. A by-product of the process of using a tooth comb on a small child's hair in a never-ending quest for lice and other creepy-crawlies picked up at school.

Seet. Applies to eyesight, which often means recourse to the glasses which are handed down in the family. Or it could be a landmark, such as York Minster or a local pub. Then it's a "seet for sore eyes".

Shelvins. Light wooden extensions to a farm cart to enable it to carry a quite large load of hay. A Dales farmer, watching his growing lad shovelling food into his mouth said: "Nay, if thou goes on eating like that we'll hev to put some shelvin's on thee plate".

Sile. A reference to rain, not the gentle sort but that which come down "like stair-rods". When it's siling down, tha knaws about it!

Sitha. Also sista, meaning "see there", as in "Sitha—thy Fred's off to t'pub agean".

Skelp. To beat a naughty child, as often happened in the old days, the prelude being the announcement that "Ah'll skept tha". The boy had his revenge when he grew bigger and stronger than Dad!

Slape. During a cold snap in winter, the roads got fearfully slape [slippery].

Smittle. To pass on a contageous or infectious dissease, as when someone says: "I've getten a cold—tha must hev smittled me".

Snap. A light meal, sandwich based (see "Jock"). A weaver complained to his wife she did not give him enough sandwiches. So cut a whole loaf in two, buttered and jammed it and stuck it together again. He said, that evening: "Tha nobbut gave me one sandwich today".

Snaw-broth. When snow begins to thaw. (The old-time postman claimed there was nothing like clogs for keeping out snaw-broth).

Sneck. A door latch. The rent-collector was known as a sneck-lifter. Sneck-lifting was when you had the price of a drink and could visit the local pub.

Speyk. A word meaning "speak", as in "Tha'll hev ta speyk up, lad, cos I haven't got my hearing aid on".

Spice. A child's favourite word, meaning sweets. A Saturday Penny secured a bag full of spice. Shrewed confectioners got rid of unwanted stock by putting it in Lucky Bags, which were sold for a penny apiece. Small children who had no money for spice teased local shopkeepers by asking for "Jelly-round-squares" and then running away.

Spuggy. The sparrow, admired because of its chirrupy call and cheerful disposition in an unpromising urban setting.

Stalled. When a person is weary or "fed up".

Starken. To stiffen (East Yorkshire). "Thou mustn't drink cowd water after chips or it'll starken the fat".

Stee. A ladder, of course. Features in a commonly respected superstition—never walk under a ladder. But when stepping from the pavement on to the road to avoid walking under a ladder, try not to knock any cars over.

Steg. A Dales word for t'owd gander, the sort that pursues you with neck outstretched, uttering a loud hissing sound.

Stubber. A large needle used in rug-making. The famous "pegged rug" was made from bits and pieces cut from the family's worn-out clothes.

Summat. It simply means "something". It might be "summat and nowt" [what's all the fuss about?] or "summat's up" [something is the matter].

Sup. To drink, applied to tea or ale. Supping-up tea usually means there's work in the offing and supping-up ale signifies the near approach of closing time.

Teea. The stuff that's really too good to be supped-up, or rushed. At a Dales farm, an invitation to have a cup of tea means a full-blown meal, with apologies that there's nowt warm.

Tewtlin. An upper Dales expression, used as the first snowflakes of an impending blizzard are falling.

Thible. A spoon for stirring poddish [porridge] which each morning gave the spine of the farmer and his men that little bit extra rigidity. "It's your stomach 'at 'ods thee back up". Poddish was covered with "blue" milk, or what was left after the cream had been skimmed off. If the men didn't fancy it, the blue milk was fed to the calves or pigs!

Thoil. A stirring Yorkshire characteristic is the ability to thoil [endure or withstand]. Also "begrudge", as in "Yon fellow can't thoil to lend owt".

Thou. Also thoo, tha and thi. It means "you", of course. The thee's and thou's in the conversation of rural Yorkshire might have emanated from the constant hearing at Sunday worship of the Authorised version of the Bible. A daleswoman who objected to her husband's prattlings was heard to say: "Doan't thee thou me!"

Thrang. Busy, or trying to do several jobs at the same time.

Titivate. To prettify, permissible in the case of a young lass on Courting Neet. Those who are always glancing in a mirror are said to be "fancying thersens".

Toppin'. A forelock, to be touched by a servant in the presence of his master. Not to be plastered with hair cream by those going to Chapel (hair cream being a product of the Devil). Incidentally, a horse has a toppin'.

Twined. In a bad mood. The afflicted person may be "as twined as a wasp" or "as twined as Dick's hat-band".

Twinter. Now we're back to sheep. A twinter is one which has experienced two winters.

Winter-'edge. A free-standing, two piece rack, also known as a clothes-horse, used for the indoor drying of clothes.

Yammer. The means incessant chatter, which is abhored in a county where the inclination is towards short, sharp sentences and long pauses. Taciturnity has been defined as "the ability to say nowt for a long time".

Yonderly. Vague. We all get "yonderly" when our minds stray. It's a lovely feeling—if you are not driving a car.

Try and unravel the following, which were culled 20 years ago from the magazine of the Airedale Hospital Management committee:

1. Nardenden, wotardooin?
2. Asta seenim ont telly?
3. Corforus arpastate itmornin.
4. It dunt marrer.
5. Lerrus gurrat pixchurs.
6. Astagorra tanner?

8. Eez gonna gerra lorre lolly forrit.
9. Lerrer gerontbus.
10. Eez nobbutta babbi.

*Onnyboddy can cure a kickin' hoss
bud them as hes yan.*